HOW TO HANDLE THE SQUID GAME OF LIFE

US MANISH

To *Mom*,

For always believing in me, even when I didn't believe in
myself.

Contents

Foreword

Hey there,

If you're holding this book, you're probably feeling a bit like Player 456 right now – lost, confused, and wondering how you ended up in this crazy game called life. Trust me, I get it. I'm right there with you, trying to make sense of it all.

You see, I'm not some life coach who's figured it all out. In fact, while writing this book, I've been going through one of the toughest phases of my own life. Breakups that felt like a brutal game of Red Light, Green Light, anxiety that's been a constant Tug of War with my mind, and the never-ending pressure to succeed in the Squid Game in our society – I've experienced it all.

So why write a book, you ask? Well, it's because I realized that even in my darkest moments, I wasn't alone. There were others out there, just like you and me, facing their own battles. And maybe... just maybe, by sharing my stories and the lessons I've learned (often the hard way), I could help someone else feeling a little less lost.

This book isn't a magic pill or a guaranteed path to happiness. It's more like a heartfelt conversation over endless cups of *chai* – a safe space where we can talk about the stuff that keeps us up

at night, the dreams that scare us, and the heartbreaks that leave us feeling like we've been eliminated.

We'll dive into the messy world of relationships, the struggle to find our place in a world that often feels like it's rigged against us, and the pressure to live up to everyone else's expectations. We'll talk about the importance of self-love, the power of resilience, and the courage to chase our dreams, even when they seem impossible.

But most importantly, we'll remind each other that even in the darkest of times, there's always a glimmer of hope. That even when we feel like we're losing, there's always a chance to turn things around. And that no matter what life throws our way, we're never truly alone.

So, let's walk on this journey together. Let's laugh, cry, learn, and grow together. Let's face the challenges head-on and emerge from the other side, stronger and wiser.

Because even in the midst of a Squid Game, we can find and create some meaning we can find joy, purpose, and the strength to create a life that's truly worth living.

Your fellow player and fellow struggler,

US Manish

Preface

Life, my brother, is a bit like a twisted game show. There are no clear rules, the stakes are high, and sometimes, it feels like everyone else is playing with a cheat code except you.

Let me clear first, that this book is just a bit refl of theme of the popular Korean web series but drastically different, If you're holding this book, chances are you've already faced your fair share of challenges. Maybe you've been knocked down by heartbreak, felt the sting of rejection, or struggled to find your place in a world that seems to constantly change the rules. Maybe you're just tired of pretending you've got it all figured out, when in reality, you're just trying to survive each day.

Trust me, I get it. I've been there – lost, confused, and wondering if I'll ever find my way out of the maze. In fact, as I write these words, I'm still navigating my own personal Squid Game. I've stumbled, fallen, and questioned everything I thought I knew about life. But through it all, I've also discovered a strength I never knew I had, a resilience that has allowed me to pick myself up and keep going, even when the odds seemed stacked against me.

That's what this book is all about – resilience, hope, and the messy, beautiful journey of figuring out who we are and what we want from life. It's not a self-help manual or a guide to instant happiness. It's more like a late-night conversation with a close friend with a cup of coffee or chai in our hands, where we share our fears, our dreams, and the lessons we've learned along the way.

We'll talk about the Red Lights and Green Lights of relationships, the Tug of War with our own minds, and the never-ending quest to find our place in a world that often feels like a chaotic Squid Game. We'll discuss the importance of self-love, the power of vulnerability, and the courage to chase our dreams, even when they seem impossible.

You'll hear stories from my own life, as well as from others who have faced similar challenges. You'll find practical tips and insights gleaned from years of therapy, self-reflection, and the occasional existential crisis. But most importantly, you'll discover that you're not alone in this journey. There are millions of us out there, navigating the same maze, trying to find our way to the finish line.

So, my friend, let's embark on this journey together. Let's laugh, cry, learn, and grow together. Let's embrace the chaos, face our fears, and celebrate our victories, no matter how small they may seem.

This book is my hand extended to you, a reminder that even in the darkest of times, there's always a glimmer of hope. Together, we can find our way out of the Squid Game and create a life that's truly worth living.

Acknowledgements

First off, a massive shout-out to my family, my Mom and Sumit – the OG players in my life. You've faced more Red Lights and Glass Bridges than anyone I know. But you always found a way to keep moving forward. Your strength and resilience are my inspirations, *Maa*. This book is yours.

To my *yaars*, my squad, my partners-in-crime – you guys are the real MVPs. Thanks for the endless *chai sessions*, the late-night pep talks, and the constant reminders that laughter is the best medicine, even when life feels like a Squid Game gone wrong. Special shoutout to *Vivek* and *Bhaskar*, who always know how to make me laugh even when I'm feeling like Player 456. You guys are the family I chose, and I'm forever grateful for your love and support.

And a special thanks to Ankit Bisht, my friend from mumbai. But wait...Thanks for what? I honestly have no clue. Even I'm scratching my head wondering why I'm including him in my acknowledgments. While I was burning the midnight sleep counting my pages, this *Praani* was busy counting his GFs and thinking of how to woo them on Snapchat, Tinder, or maybe...just maybe, straight to Oyo... Anyway.

Ankit, if I write any romantic bestseller like: "How to Handle the Dating Games of Life," you'll be getting a whole chapter or becoming the co-author. Well, it's time for you to go and figure out Oyo's best deals.

And to that certain someone who tried their best to ruin my life & played the villain in my story, but congratulations ! you failed miserably, thanks for the unintentional motivation. You might have thought you were breaking & hurting me, but you actually made me stronger.

Finally, a massive thank you to Vipin Yadav, the editor of this book, you framed this book into shape. Your keen eye for detail and unwavering support turned my wandering thoughts into a coherent project. thank you for your patience, your wisdom, and your unwavering belief in this project. You've helped me shape this book into something I'm truly proud of, and I couldn't have done it without you. Your red pen is mightier than any sword, and your feedback has been invaluable in making this book the best it can be. And yes, the missing one Pawan. There is nothing more for you, just one thing: *"HAR BAAT PE TAANG NAHI ADAATE BETA"*

And yes ! a huge thank to *Shiva,* the head of our *"Guptchar Vibhaag"* for always working harder for the squad and keep an eye on everything happening around. And to every member of the Squad who is ready for *JASOOSI* even in midnight just for a Samosa and some *Gol-Gappe.*

To my readers – you're the reason I poured my heart and soul into these pages. I hope this book resonates with you, makes you laugh, cry, and maybe even inspires you to face your own challenges with renewed courage and determination. Remember, we're all in this crazy game together, and we've got each other's backs.

And finally, to the universe – thanks for throwing me so many lemons, though i found it enough harder to make *Shikanji* of that as they haven't always been easy to catch, but they've definitely taught me a thing or two about resilience, perseverance, and the importance of never giving up.

So, here's to all of you – the players, the dreamers, the fighters, the survivors. May we all find the strength to navigate this Squid Game of life with grace, humor, and an unwavering belief in ourselves.

Prologue

Life's a game, they say. But sometimes, it feels less like a friendly round of Ludo and more like a twisted, high-stakes Squid Game. You know, the kind where the rules are rigged, the challenges are brutal, and the results are horror.

The thing is, we don't sign up for this game. We're thrown into it, unprepared and often ill-equipped. We're forced to navigate a maze of obstacles – heartbreak, loss, betrayal, failure – with no clear map or instructions. And just when we think we've finally found our footing, life throws us another curveball, another challenge that threatens to knock us off our game.

I know this all too well. I've been there, in the trenches, battling the demons of self-doubt, wrestling with grief, and staring down the barrel of financial ruin. I've felt the sting of rejection, the agony of loss, and the crushing weight of despair.

But I've also discovered that even in the darkest of times, there's a flicker of hope, a spark of resilience that refuses to be extinguished. It's that spark that led me to write this book, a testament to the human spirit's ability to endure, adapt, and ultimately triumph.

This isn't a fairy tale with a guaranteed happy ending. It's a raw, honest, and sometimes uncomfortable look at the challenges we all face. It's about the messy, complicated reality of life, the struggles we endure, and the lessons we learn along the way.

But it's also a story of hope, a reminder that even when we feel like we're losing, there's always a chance for a comeback. It's a call to action, a challenge to rise above our circumstances and create a life that's truly worth living.

So, if you're feeling lost, overwhelmed, or like you're about to be eliminated from the game, take a deep breath and join me on this journey. Let's explore the twists and turns of the Squid Game of life together, and discover the hidden strengths that lie within us.

Because even in the face of adversity, we have the power to choose our own path, to rewrite our own story, and to emerge as the victors of our own lives.

CHAPTER ONE

GAME OVER? BUT LIFE'S NOT

The BDTS-FBD express 22444 chugged into the station, its brakes screeching like a rusty record finally skipping to a stop. I stepped off the train, an optimist traveler returning home after a long and difficult journey. As I inhaled the familiar scent of dust and diesel, a wave of relief washed over me. I had made it back, bruised but not broken, ready to start anew.

My life had been derailed since childhood, a series of "wrongs and rights", Ups and downs, that had left me feeling lost and adrift. But this time, I was determined to get back on track. I had a plan, a vision for a brighter future, a fresh start that would finally allow me to live the life I had always dreamed of.

The first few days back home were filled with a renewed sense of optimism. I reconnected with childhood friends, sharing stories and laughter over endless cups of chai. I spent time with family and all the *jasoos* friends (Who always keep me informed about what's happening throughout our area and village), basking in their unconditional love and support. I even started exploring new career opportunities, determined to find a path that would finally lead to fulfillment. It felt like a weight had been lifted from my shoulders, like I had finally broken free from the shackles of my past.

But then, the phone rang. It was the *Lekhpal*, the village revenue official, his voice curt and dismissive. "I'm calling to inform you that you've lost your case," he said. "The land is no longer yours."

My heart plummeted. The agricultural land, a vital source of income for my family for generations, was now in jeopardy. The land we had toiled on, nurtured, and depended on was being ripped away from us.

In a matter of days, my world turned upside down. The savings I had painstakingly accumulated over the years were poured into legal fees, leaving me with nothing but a mountain of debt and a crushing sense of defeat. The future I had envisioned, the fresh start I had craved, seemed like a distant mirage, fading with each passing day.

The weight of it all became unbearable. I couldn't eat, couldn't sleep, couldn't focus on anything but the looming threat of financial ruin. The familiar demons of self-doubt and anxiety reared their ugly heads, whispering in my ear that I was a failure, a burden to my family, a loser in the game of life.

And then, as if the universe hadn't dealt me enough cruel blows, fate delivered its final punch. My father collapsed one morning, clutching his chest. The frantic rush to the hospital, the sterile smell of medicines with the bitter taste of fear, and the endless hours of waiting, punctuated by hushed and scary conversations and the scary beeping of machines, are etched into my memory like a tattoo.

When the doctor emerged from the ICU, his face a mask of grim shape, I knew it was over. The world seemed to tilt on its axis as he uttered the words I had dreaded most: "We did everything we could, but..."

The rest of his sentence faded into a meaningless drone as I stumbled back, my legs buckling beneath me. The hospital walls closed in, I sank onto a cold plastic chair, my body wracked with sobs.

In that moment, I felt utterly helpless. The world had turned its back on me, snatching away my hopes, my dreams, and my...my everything. A black hole threatening to swallow me whole.

I had lost almost everything – my land, my savings, my father. The game was over, and I had lost. Or so I thought.

In the aftermath of my father's death, I found myself trapped in a vicious cycle of grief and despair. I was imprisoned in my own home, unable to venture out for work or solace. The legal battle for our land raged on, demanding my constant attention and draining what little energy I had left.

Each day felt like a cruel game of Tug of War, my mind and body locked in a relentless struggle for survival. On one side, the gnawing fear of financial ruin, the constant worry about how I would support my family and continue the fight for our land. On the other side, the crushing weight of grief, the agonizing emptiness left by my father's absence.

I was caught in a catch-22: I needed to work to earn money to fight the case, but I couldn't leave home to work because the case demanded my constant presence. The days blurred into a monotonous routine of court hearings, endless paperwork, and sleepless nights filled with worry and despair.

I felt like a prisoner in my own home, the walls closing in on me with each passing day. The outside world, with its bustling markets, vibrant colors, and endless possibilities, seemed like a distant memory, a fading dream.

The relentless ticking of the clock echoed through the sterile hospital corridors, each tick a painful reminder of time slipping away, of opportunities lost, of dreams shattered. I sat slumped in the plastic chair, the harsh fluorescent lights casting a sickly glow on my tear-stained face. The doctor's words, "We did everything we could, but..." reverberated in my ears, a cruel echo of the finality of death.

Lost in a fog of grief and despair, I couldn't shake the feeling that I had failed, not just my father, but myself. I had returned home with the promise of a new beginning, only to be plunged into a deeper abyss than I had ever known.

The events of the past few months had left me feeling like a contestant in a twisted, real-life version of the Squid Game. Each challenge, each setback, felt like a cruel test of my resilience, my sanity, my will to survive. The land dispute, the financial ruin, the loss of my father – it was as if the universe had orchestrated a series of sadistic games, designed to break my spirit and leave me defeated.

And now, trapped in the labyrinth of my own grief, I was faced with a crucial question: Was this the end of my game? Or was it merely the beginning of a new, even more challenging round?

The answer, my friend, depends on how you choose to see it. For, as the title of this book suggests, "How to Handle the Squid Game of Life," it's up to you to decide whether it's a question or an answer. Is it a lament over the unfairness of life's challenges, or a call to action, a reminder that even in the darkest of times, we have the power to choose our own path?

My story, as you've just read, is one of loss, grief, and seemingly insurmountable obstacles. But it's also a story of resilience, of the unyielding human spirit that refuses to be defeated, even in the face of overwhelming adversity.

Like the players in the Squid Game, we are all faced with choices. We can succumb to fear, give in to despair, and allow ourselves to be eliminated. Or we can rise to the challenge, tap into our inner strength, and fight for our survival.

The games we face may be different – some of us battle financial hardship, others grapple with illness or loss, while still others struggle with the demons of addiction or mental illness. But the underlying principle remains the same: life is a series of challenges, and it's up to us to decide how we will play the game.

We can choose to be victims, blaming our circumstances for our misfortunes. Or we can choose to be warriors, taking ownership of our lives and fighting for the future we deserve.

We can choose to wallow in self-pity, allowing our failures to define us. Or we can choose to learn from our mistakes, grow from our experiences, and emerge stronger than ever before.

We can choose to isolate ourselves, believing that we are alone in our struggles. Or we can choose to reach out to others, find support in our communities, and build a network of allies who will help us weather the storms of life.

The choice, is yours. Will you let the game defeat you? Or will you rise to the challenge and become the master of your own destiny?

Remember, even in the darkest of nights, the stars still shine. Even in the depths of despair, there is always hope. And even when it feels like the game is over, there's always a chance for a comeback.

It's in those moments of utter despair, when the world seems to be conspiring against us, that we discover our true strength. It's when we're backed into a corner, stripped of our illusions and comforts, that we're forced to confront the raw truth of our existence. And it's in that confrontation that we find the seeds of resilience, the spark of hope that ignites the fire within us.

But let's be clear: this isn't some feel-good story about miraculously overcoming adversity and achieving overnight success. It's about the messy, painful, and often frustrating process of rebuilding your life, brick by brick, after it's been shattered into a million pieces.

It's about facing your demons head-on, acknowledging your pain, and refusing to let it consume you. It's about finding the courage to ask for help, to lean on your loved ones, and to accept that you don't have to go through this alone.

It's about embracing the uncertainty of the future, the unknown path that stretches before you, and taking that first tentative step forward, even when you're not sure where it will lead.

And it's about recognizing that even in the darkest of times, there are still moments of joy, of beauty, of connection to be found. It might be a warm smile from a stranger, a breathtaking sunset, or a simple act of kindness that reminds you that the world isn't all doom and gloom.

So, if you're feeling like you're stuck in your own personal Squid Game, I want you to know that you're not alone. There are countless others who have faced similar challenges, who have felt the sting of loss and the weight of despair. But they've also found a way to rise above it, to find meaning in their pain, and to create a life that's worth living.

This book is my attempt to share the lessons I've learned on my own tumultuous journey. It's a guidebook for navigating the challenges of life, a roadmap for finding your way back from the brink of despair, and a reminder that even when it feels like the game is over, there's always a chance for a comeback.

So, my friend, if you're ready to take that first step, to face your fears, to embrace the unknown, then turn the page and let's embark on this journey together. Remember, you're not just a player in this game – you're the author of your own story.

Consider the story of Sudha Murthy, the renowned Indian author and philanthropist. Born into a modest family, she faced numerous obstacles on her path to success. From gender discrimination to financial hardships, she encountered countless "Red Lights" that threatened to derail her dreams. But with unwavering determination and a refusal to accept defeat, she persevered, eventually becoming a role model for millions of young women in India.

Or take the inspiring example of Arunima Sinha, the first female amputee to climb Mount Everest. After losing her leg in a tragic accident, she could have easily succumbed to despair. But instead, she channeled her grief into determination, training tirelessly to achieve the seemingly impossible. Her story is a testament to the indomitable human spirit, a shining example of what can be accomplished when we refuse to give up on our dreams.

These are just two examples of countless individuals who have faced their own personal Squid Games and emerged victorious. Their stories remind us that even when the odds seem stacked against us, we always have a choice. We can choose to give up, to wallow in self-pity, to let our circumstances define us. Or we can choose to fight back, to rise above the challenges, and to create a life that is both meaningful and fulfilling.

So, if you're feeling overwhelmed, lost, or like you're constantly one step away from elimination, remember this: you are not alone. There are others who have walked this path before you, who have faced their own demons and emerged stronger on the other side.

Take a moment to reflect on your own life. What challenges are you facing? What obstacles are standing in your way? What dreams have you been putting off for fear of failure?

Now, imagine yourself as a player in the Squid Game. How would you approach these challenges? What strategies would you use to overcome them? How would you tap into your inner strength and resilience?

Think of the games themselves: Each one is a microcosm of life's challenges, requiring a unique combination of skills and strategies to survive. Red Light, Green Light teaches us the importance of patience and self-control in a world that constantly urges us to rush. The Dalgona Candy challenge demands precision and attention to detail, reminding us that even the smallest misstep can have serious consequences. The Tug of War game emphasizes the power of teamwork and collaboration, highlighting the importance of building strong relationships and support systems.

And what about the glass bridge? It's a terrifying metaphor for the risks we must take in life, the leaps of faith we must make in order to achieve our goals. Sometimes, the path ahead is uncertain, and the only way forward is to trust our instincts and take a chance. We may stumble, we may fall, but even in failure, there are valuable lessons to be learned.

But perhaps the most important lesson of the Squid Game is this: even in the face of seemingly insurmountable odds, there is always a chance for a comeback. Just when you think the game is over, a new opportunity may present itself, a hidden strength may emerge, a chance encounter may change the course of your life.

Think about it this way: if Player 456, a debt-ridden gambler with a seemingly hopeless future, can emerge as the victor of the Squid Game, then surely we, too, can overcome the challenges that life throws our way.

The key is to approach these challenges with the same mindset as a Squid Game player: resourcefulness, determination, and a willingness to learn and adapt. We must be willing to take risks, to embrace uncertainty, and to learn from our mistakes.

But most importantly, we must never give up hope. Even when the odds seem stacked against us, even when we feel like we've lost everything, there is always a chance for a comeback. We may not always win, but we can always learn, grow, and become stronger in the process.

So, the next time you find yourself facing a seemingly insurmountable obstacle, remember the lessons of the Squid Game. Take a deep breath, assess the situation, and devise a strategy. Reach out to your allies, tap into your hidden strengths, and never give up on your dreams.

It's a game, alright. A game where the rules are rigged, the odds stacked against us, and the stakes impossibly high. But it's also a game where the most unexpected players can rise to the occasion, where hidden strengths can be revealed, and where the human spirit can triumph over even the most daunting challenges.

Life, like the Squid Game, is a test of resilience, a trial by fire that forces us to confront our deepest fears and insecurities. It's a journey filled with twists and turns, setbacks and triumphs, moments of despair and flashes of brilliance. And just like the players in the game, we have the power to choose our own path, to write our own ending.

We can choose to succumb to the darkness, to allow our failures and losses to define us. Or we can choose to rise above the ashes, to find meaning in our pain, and to create a new narrative for ourselves.

We can choose to play the game on someone else's terms, following the rules that have been set for us. Or we can choose to rewrite the rules, to forge our own path, and to create a game that reflects our own values and aspirations.

The choice is ours, my friend. Will you let the game defeat you? Or will you rise to the challenge and become the master of your own destiny?

As I stood at my father's graveside, the weight of my grief threatening to crush me, I made a decision. I would not allow the pain of loss to consume me. Instead, I would channel that pain into fuel, a burning desire to create a better future for myself and my family.

The road ahead would be long and arduous, filled with obstacles and setbacks. But I was no longer a scared child lost in the woods. I was a warrior, forged in the crucible of adversity, ready to face whatever life threw my way.

I would not let the game defeat me. I would fight untill the last breath.

CHAPTER TWO

PLAYER 456 TO PLAYER 1: YOUR COMEBACK

Ever been knocked down so hard you felt like life had hit the "Game Over" button on you? I have. I've been that crumpled ?500 note, lying forgotten in the gutter, wondering how I got there and if I'd ever be worth anything again. The kind of loss I'm talking about, it's not just losing a round of Ludo or missing the last train home. It's the kind that leaves a gaping hole in your soul, the kind that makes you question everything you thought you knew about yourself and the world around you.

But here's the thing, *Dost:* even the most crumpled note can be smoothed out, given a second chance, a new lease on life. And so can you. This chapter isn't about pretending that pain doesn't exist, or that bouncing back is as easy as flipping a switch. It's about acknowledging the struggle, embracing the messiness, and finding the courage to rise from the ashes, stronger and wiser than before.

Think of it like this: life is a game of snakes and ladders. We all start at the bottom, full of hope and ambition, eager to climb to the top. But along the way, we inevitably encounter snakes that send us tumbling back down. The loss of a loved one, a financial setback, a broken heart – these are the snakes that can derail our progress, leaving us feeling bruised and defeated.

But here's the secret, the one they don't teach you in school: those snakes are also opportunities in disguise. They force us to re-evaluate our path, to learn from our mistakes, and to emerge from the darkness with a newfound appreciation for the ladders that can lift us up.

Maybe you're wondering, "How can I possibly turn things around? I've lost so much, I'm so far behind." Trust me, I've asked myself the same questions countless times. But then I remember the stories of those who have overcome seemingly insurmountable odds, the underdogs who defied expectations and achieved the impossible.

Think of J.K. Rowling, who went from being a struggling single mother on welfare to a bestselling author whose books have touched millions of lives. Or Oprah Winfrey, who overcame a childhood of poverty and abuse to become a media mogul and one of the most influential people in the world.

These stories remind us that even when we feel like Player 456, down on our luck and out of options, there's always a chance for a comeback. It's about tapping into our inner strength, our resilience, our unwavering belief in ourselves. It's about refusing to let our past define our future, and instead, choosing to write our own fate, one chapter at a time.

So, how do you go from Player 456, the underdog, to Player 1, the champion of your own life? It starts with a shift in perspective. It's about seeing your struggles not as punishments but as opportunities for growth, not as full stops but as commas in the ongoing sentence of your life.

Think of it like a Bollywood masala movie. The hero always faces setbacks, heartbreaks, and seemingly insurmountable odds. But he never gives up. He digs deep, finds his inner strength, and ultimately emerges victorious, often with a killer dance number to boot.

Now, I'm not saying you need to break into a choreographed routine every time life throws you a lemon (although, hey, it might help!). But what I am saying is that you have the power to rewrite your own script. You can choose to be the hero of your own story, the one who overcomes challenges, learns from mistakes, and ultimately triumphs.

It starts with taking ownership of your life. Instead of blaming external factors for your misfortunes, look inward and ask yourself, "What can I do to change this situation?" Maybe it's learning a new skill, starting a side hustle, or seeking professional help for your mental health. Whatever it is, take that first step, even if it's a small one. Remember, even the longest journey begins with a single step.

And don't be afraid to ask for help. Just like in the Squid Game, alliances can be crucial for survival. Talk to your friends, family, therapist, or anyone who can offer a listening ear and a helping hand. Sharing your burdens can lighten the load and provide you with the support you need to keep moving forward.

Remember, this isn't about achieving perfection. It's about progress. It's about celebrating small victories, learning from your mistakes, and never giving up on yourself. Just like a crumpled ?500 note, you may be a bit worn and torn, but you still have value.

The path from Player 456 to Player 1 is not a straight line. It's more like a Mumbai auto-rickshaw ride – bumpy, unpredictable, and often filled with unexpected detours. But just like that auto-rickshaw driver who somehow manages to navigate the chaotic streets of Mumbai, you too can find your way through the maze of life's challenges.

It starts with acceptance. Accepting that life isn't always fair, that sometimes the bad guys win, and that even the best-laid plans can go awry. It's about recognizing that setbacks and failures are not a reflection of your worth, but rather an opportunity to learn, grow, and become a stronger version of yourself.

It's also about finding your tribe, your gang, your squad – the people who will cheer you on, offer a shoulder to cry on, and remind you that you're not alone in this crazy game called life. Think of them as your personal cheerleaders, your support system, your very own "Frontbenchers" who will always have your back.

And finally, it's about finding your passion, your "IKIGAI" your reason for waking up in the morning. It might be a hobby you've always loved, a cause you're passionate about, or a dream you've been putting off for far too long. Whatever it is, pursue it with all your heart. It's in those moments of pure joy and fulfillment that we truly come alive, that we shed our Player 456 status and become the Player 1 we were always meant to be.

So, what are you waiting for? It's time to dust yourself off, put on your game face, and step back into the arena. Remember, the game isn't over until you say it is. And even then, there's always a chance for a sequel, a redemption arc, a new beginning.

The comeback isn't a one-size-fits-all formula. It's as unique as your fingerprints, as varied as the spices in a *biryani.* For some, it might mean starting a new business venture, like a chaiwallah who dreams of owning a chain of cafes. For others, it might involve healing a broken heart, piece by piece, like a kintsugi artist mending a shattered pot with gold. And for some, it might simply mean finding the courage to get out of bed in the morning and face another day.

But no matter what form your comeback takes, there are a few universal truths that can guide you along the way. First, remember that you are not your circumstances. Just because you've been dealt a bad hand doesn't mean you're destined to lose the game. Life is full of second chances, third chances, even fourth chances. It's never too late to turn things around.

Second, embrace your vulnerabilities. Don't try to be someone you're not, or pretend that everything is okay when it's not. Allow yourself to feel the pain, the anger, the frustration. But don't let those emotions define you. Instead, use them as fuel to propel you forward, to motivate you to create a better future.

Third, surround yourself with positive people. Just like in the game of Antakshari, where you need a team to support you and help you remember the lyrics, you need a tribe of people who will lift you up, cheer you on, and remind you of your worth. These are the people who will help you through the tough times, who will celebrate your victories, and who will always believe in you, even when you don't believe in yourself.

Fourth, don't be afraid to ask for help. Sometimes, we need a helping hand to get back on our feet, a guiding light to show us the way. It could be a therapist, a mentor, a friend, or even a stranger who offers a kind word or a listening ear. Remember, it takes courage to ask for help, but it's a sign of strength, not weakness.

And finally, never give up on your dreams. They may seem far-fetched, impossible even, but don't let that deter you. Dreams are what keep us going, what give our lives meaning and purpose. So hold on to them tightly, nurture them, and never stop believing in their power to transform your life.

The road to comeback Is not easy. It's a winding path filled with potholes and detours. But with each step you take, with each obstacle you overcome, you'll discover a newfound strength, a resilience you never knew you had. And one day, you'll look back on your journey and realize that it was in those moments of struggle, those darkest of nights, that you truly found yourself.

Speaking of comebacks, let me tell you about my friend, Rakul. Now, Rakul wasn't exactly known for his academic prowess. He was the kind of guy who'd spend more time doodling in his notebook than actually studying. He failed his 10th-grade board exams not once, but twice. His parents were mortified, his teachers were exasperated, and his friends, well, they were used to it.

But Rakul had a secret weapon: his infectious sense of humor. He could make anyone laugh, even in the most dire of circumstances. And he used that humor to cope with his failures, to deflect the criticism, and to keep his spirits up.

One night, after a particularly brutal round of exam results and a few too many beers, Rakul and his friends gathered on a rooftop. The mood was somber, the weight of Rakul's academic struggles hanging heavy in the air.

Suddenly, in a moment of drunken inspiration, Rakul stumbled to his feet, his eyes gleaming with mischief. "Alright, listen up, guys!" he slurred, adopting a stern demeanor and a comically exaggerated voice. "Today, we shall delve into the fascinating world of... quadratic equations!"

His friends erupted In laughter, recognizing the all-too-familiar drone of their math teacher, Mr. Mathur. Rakul continued, pacing back and forth, scribbling nonsensical equations on an imaginary chalkboard.

"Now, remember, class," Rakul-as-Mr. Mathur chimed, "the key to solving these quadratic conundrums lies in the mystical formula... minus b plus or minus the square root of b squared minus four ac, all divided by two a!"

Rakul's friends were in stitches, rolling on the floor with laughter. He had captured Mr. Mathur's quirks perfectly, from his exaggerated hand gestures to his tendency to drool slightly when explaining complex concepts.

Encouraged by their reaction, Rakul morphed into one Bollywood star after another, his impersonations growing increasingly outrageous and hilarious. His friends were in stitches, their rooftop becoming a makeshift comedy club. It was in that moment, amidst the laughter and camaraderie, that Rakul stumbled upon a talent he never knew he had: mimicry.

Soon, word of Rakul's talent spread like wildfire. He was invited to perform at weddings, parties, and even corporate events. His career as a mimic took off, and before he knew it, he was making more money than most of his "successful" classmates.

Rakul's story is a reminder that sometimes, our greatest weaknesses can turn out to be our greatest strengths. It's about finding that unique spark within ourselves, that hidden talent that can lead us to unexpected success.

It's about embracing our quirks, our flaws, and our imperfections, and using them to create a life that is both meaningful and fulfilling. Rakul's journey wasn't a straight line to success. He faced numerous rejections and setbacks along the way. There were nights when he doubted himself, when the laughter seemed to fade away, replaced by the echo of his past failures.

But Rakul never gave up. He drew strength from his friends, his family, and his unwavering belief in himself. He used every rejection as an opportunity to learn and grow, refining his craft and expanding his repertoire of impersonations. He learned to embrace his "Pappu-ness," turning his perceived weaknesses into strengths.

Rakul's resilience paid off. He started getting booked for bigger events, his reputation as a hilarious and versatile mimic growing with each performance. He even landed a gig on a popular comedy show, captivating audiences across the nation with his spot-on impersonations and infectious energy.

His success wasn't just about financial gain; it was about finding his purpose, his passion. Rakul realized that his gift of laughter had the power to heal, to connect, and to inspire. He used his platform to spread joy, to bring people together, and to remind everyone that even in the face of adversity, laughter can be the ultimate comeback.

So, if you're feeling like a failure, like you'll never amount to anything, remember Rakul. Remember that even the most unlikely of us can achieve extraordinary things, if only we're willing to embrace our true selves and follow our passions.

The comeback Isn't about becoming someone you're not. It's about rediscovering who you are, deep down, beneath the layers of self-doubt and societal expectations. It's about finding your own voice, your own rhythm, your own unique way of dancing to the beat of your own dhol.

Rakul's journey teaches us that life isn't always about following the straight and narrow path. Sometimes, the detours, the unexpected twists and turns, lead us to our true calling. It's about embracing our inner "Rakul," the part of us that's quirky, unconventional, and unafraid to stand out.

Life's grand stage isn't always a smooth performance. There will be missed cues, forgotten lines, and the occasional pratfall. But just as a seasoned actor finds their footing after a stumble, so too can we transform our missteps into a captivating comeback.

The path to success isn't always a linear trajectory. Sometimes, it's a winding road with unexpected detours, hidden shortcuts, and unforeseen obstacles. Embracing these twists and turns, these seemingly insignificant moments of serendipity, is where the true magic of transformation lies.

The world often tells us to conform, to fit into neat little boxes labeled "success" or "failure." But true fulfillment lies in breaking free from those constraints, in embracing our unique quirks and imperfections. It's in those moments of vulnerability, when we dare to be ourselves, that we discover our hidden talents and untapped potential.

Imagine a life where your perceived weaknesses become your greatest strengths, where your stumbling blocks transform into stepping stones. Imagine a life where laughter, even in the face of adversity, becomes your secret weapon, a beacon of hope that guides you towards your comeback.

It's not about erasing your past failures or pretending they never happened. It's about acknowledging them, learning from them, and using them as fuel to propel you forward. It's about rewriting the script, turning your "Game

Over" into a thrilling new chapter filled with unexpected twists and turns.

Remember, the power to change your story lies within you. Embrace your individuality, cultivate your passions, and never stop believing in your ability to rise above any challenge. Because just like the phoenix rising from the ashes, you too can transform your setbacks into a spectacular comeback, a testament to the indomitable spirit that resides within you.

So, if you find yourself standing at a crossroads, facing a seemingly insurmountable obstacle, take a deep breath and remember the power of your own story. It's not over yet. This is just the beginning of your grand comeback, your chance to show the world the true strength and resilience that lies within you.

Life's grand stage is not merely a series of successes and failures, but a continuous performance where every act, every scene, contributes to the unfolding narrative. It is in the quiet moments of introspection, the times when the applause fades and the spotlight dims, that we find the true essence of our being.

It's not about being the most talented, the most intelligent, or the most successful. It's about discovering the unique gifts that reside within, the hidden talents that lie dormant, waiting to be awakened. It's about embracing the parts of ourselves that we've been taught to hide, the quirks and idiosyncrasies that make us who we are.

Imagine a life where your perceived flaws become your most cherished assets, where your vulnerabilities transform into sources of strength. Imagine a life where laughter, even in the face of adversity, becomes your guiding light, illuminating the path towards your true potential.

The comeback Is not a singular event, but a continuous journey of self-discovery, growth, and reinvention. It's about challenging the status quo, defying expectations, and forging your own path. It's about embracing the unknown with open arms, knowing that every twist and turn holds the potential for transformation.

Don't let the fear of failure hold you back. Embrace the inevitable setbacks as opportunities for growth, as stepping stones towards a more fulfilling life. Remember, even the darkest night eventually gives way to the dawn.

The power to create your own narrative lies within you. You are the author of your own story, the director of your own play. Don't let anyone else dictate your destiny. Take the reins, embrace your unique voice, and create a masterpiece that reflects the true essence of your being.Rakul's journey wasn't an overnight transformation; it was a gradual blossoming, a patient unfolding of his true potential. He didn't magically become a mimicry maestro; it was a process of trial and error, of countless hours spent honing his craft, of pushing his boundaries and venturing outside his comfort zone.

He fac'd rejection and ridicule, but he never let those setbacks define him. Instead, he used them as fuel to ignite his determination, to push himself to greater heights. He learned that failure wasn't the end, but merely a detour on the winding road to success.

Rakul's story teaches us that our greatest setbacks can become our most valuable assets. It's in the depths of despair that we discover our true strength, our resilience, and our unwavering spirit. It's in the face of adversity that we find our voice, our purpose, and our unique gifts.

But the comeback isn't just about overcoming obstacles; it's about embracing the journey, with all its twists and turns, its highs and lows. It's about finding joy in the process, celebrating the small victories, and learning from the missteps.

It's about understanding that success isn't a destination but a continuous journey of self-discovery, growth, and reinvention. It's about pushing your boundaries, challenging your limits, and daring to be different. It's about embracing your inner "Pappu," the part of you that's playful, unconventional, and unafraid to stand out.

And most importantly, it's about never giving up on yourself, even when the world tells you to. It's about believing in your own potential, even when others doubt you. It's about trusting your instincts, following your passions, and creating a life that is uniquely yours.

Because just like Rakul, you have the power to turn your setbacks into stepping stones, your failures into fuel, and your Game Over into a resounding victory. Your comeback story is waiting to be written. It's time to step onto the stage, embrace your spotlight, and show the world what you're truly capable of.

The path to redemption is paved with self-belief, resilience, and the audacity to embrace your own unique brand of brilliance. It's about transforming your perceived flaws into badges of honor, your vulnerabilities into sources of strength. It's about recognizing that every stumble, every fall, is simply a stepping stone on the path to greatness.

Remember, the game of life is not about winning or losing; it's about playing with heart, with passion, and with an unwavering belief in your own potential. It's about daring to be different, to challenge the status quo, and to write your own rules.

So, if you find yourself facing a seemingly insurmountable challenge, if you feel like the world has dealt you a losing hand, take a deep breath and remember:

- **You are not defined by your past failures, but by your present actions and future aspirations.**
- **You are not alone in your struggles; millions of others are fighting their own battles, searching for their own comeback.**
- **You have the power to change your narrative, to rewrite your story, and to emerge from the ashes stronger than ever before.**

The comeback is not a destination, but a journey. It's a continuous process of growth, self-discovery, and reinvention. It's about embracing the unknown, facing your fears, and daring to dream big.

So, take that first step, however small it may seem. Embrace your inner "Pappu," the part of you that's quirky, unconventional, and unafraid to stand out. Unleash your passions, pursue your dreams, and never give up on yourself.

Because your comeback story is waiting to be written. It's a story of resilience, determination, and the unwavering belief that you can achieve anything you set your mind to. It's a story that will inspire others, uplift your spirit, and remind you that even in the darkest of times, there's always hope for a brighter tomorrow.

So, go out there and make your comeback a story worth telling, a story that will echo through the ages, a story that will remind the world that the human spirit is indomitable, that the power of transformation lies within each and every one of us.

CHAPTER THREE

RED LIGHT ON LOVE, GREEN LIGHT ON MOVING ON

Love, *yaar*. It's like that one Bollywood movie with all the drama, the mushy songs, and the inevitable heartbreak scene in the rain. We've all seen it, we've all felt it. It's a rollercoaster ride that leaves you breathless, exhilarated, and sometimes, completely messed up.

Think about it, na? You meet this amazing person, sparks fly, and you're convinced they're the one. You daydream about romantic dates, cheesy love songs, and a happily ever after straight out of a *Karan Johar* film. But then, BAM! Reality hits you like a speeding truck. Maybe they ghost you, cheat on you, or simply realize you're not their "type." Ouch.

It's like playing Red Light, Green Light with your heart. One moment you're sprinting towards love, the next you're frozen in fear, waiting for the inevitable bullet. It's a game we all play, hoping to win the grand prize of true love, but often ending up with a consolation prize of tears and a tub of ice cream.

But hey, that's life, right? It's not always going to be a Bollywood romance. Sometimes, it's more like *Mirzapur*, full of unexpected twists, turns, and bloody betrayals. But just like in those movies, even the most gut-wrenching heartbreaks can lead to epic comebacks.

So, if you're stuck in a relationship that feels more like a horror movie than a rom-com, it's time to hit the brakes. Don't be afraid to walk away from a love that's sucking the life out of you. Trust your gut, listen to your friends (especially that one friend who always gives the best advice), and have the courage to move on.

Remember, yaar, there are plenty of fish in the sea. And even if you've been burned before, don't let that stop you from diving back in. Because sometimes, the greatest love stories are the ones that start with a broken heart.

So, chin up, put on your favorite playlist, and get back in the game. Who knows, your next love story might just be a blockbuster hit.

A couple of years ago, I fell head over heels for a girl named Rashmi. We were inseparable, spending countless hours together, laughing, dreaming, and building a world of our own.

But as quickly as our love blossomed, it withered. Rashmi's affections shifted towards another guy, someone I considered a rival, a thorn in my side. The betrayal cut deep, and I spiraled into a dark abyss of depression.

Days turned into nights as I obsessively stalked their social media profiles, analyzing every post, every comment, every like. Every notification felt like a stab in the heart, a reminder of what I had lost. I became a prisoner of my own mind, trapped in a cycle of self-pity and resentment. I neglected my health, my work, and my relationships, consumed by the toxic venom of heartbreak.

But letting go wasn't as simple as deleting a few contacts or unfollowing some accounts. The memories, the what-ifs, the lingering feelings – they clung to me like a stubborn shadow.

There were nights I'd wake up in a cold sweat, the ghost of Rashmi's laughter echoing in my ears. The image of her hand intertwined with his, the rival I never wanted to acknowledge, burned into my mind. I couldn't escape the constant barrage of thoughts: "What if I had done things differently? What if I had been more attentive, more understanding?"

Days turned into a blur of restless nights and anxious days. I found myself scrolling endlessly through social media, even though I had deleted her accounts. I'd search for her name on Truecaller, hoping to catch a glimpse of her new life, her new love.

My obsession became an addiction, a toxic habit that consumed my every waking moment. I neglected my work, my studies, and my friends. I stopped going to the gym, opting instead to wallow in self-pity on my couch. My health deteriorated, my energy levels plummeted, and my once vibrant spirit dwindled into a flicker.

I knew I was self-destructing, but I couldn't stop. It was like a dark cloud had descended upon me, casting a shadow over every aspect of my life. The pain was relentless, the heartache unbearable. I felt like I was drowning in a sea of despair, with no lifeboat in sight.

It was In this moment of utter desperation that I realized I needed help. I couldn't continue down this path of self-destruction. I had to find a way to break free from the clutches of this toxic obsession. With trembling hands, I reached out to a therapist, a decision that felt both terrifying and liberating. It was a step towards acknowledging my pain, my vulnerability, and my need for support. It was a declaration that I was ready to fight for my own happiness, to reclaim my life from the clutches of despair.

Therapy became my sanctuary, a safe space where I could unravel the tangled threads of my emotions. With the help of my therapist, I began to understand the root of my obsession, the underlying insecurities that had fueled my destructive behavior.

I realized that my desperate attempts to cling to Rashmi were not born out of love, but out of fear. Fear of being alone, fear of rejection, fear of not being good enough. It was a revelation that shook me to my core, a painful truth that I had to confront.

Through therapy, I learned to challenge those negative thoughts, to replace them with positive affirmations and self-compassion. I learned to forgive myself for my mistakes, my shortcomings, and my perceived failures. I learned to embrace my imperfections, to celebrate my strengths, and to love myself unconditionally.

The process was slow, often painful, but it was also incredibly liberating. As I shed the layers of self-doubt and resentment, I discovered a newfound sense of self-worth and inner peace. I realized that my happiness didn't depend on someone else's love, but on my own self-acceptance and self-love.

With each passing day, I felt a weight lifting off my shoulders. The dark cloud that had once enveloped my life began to dissipate, replaced by a glimmer of hope. I started to see the world through a new lens, one that was brighter, more colorful, and full of possibilities.

I reconnected with my friends, who had patiently stood by me through my darkest hours. I poured myself into my work, finding solace and satisfaction in my accomplishments. I even started dating again, this time with a newfound sense of clarity and confidence.

It wasn't always smooth sailing. There were moments of doubt, setbacks, and even relapses. But I learned to be patient with myself, to forgive myself for my imperfections, and to keep moving forward.

Looking back, I realize that my heartbreak was not a curse, but a blessing in disguise. It forced me to confront my deepest fears, to heal old wounds, and to emerge stronger, wiser, and more self-assured.

I learned that sometimes, the greatest heartbreaks can lead to the greatest breakthroughs. It's in the depths of despair that we discover our true strength, our resilience, and our unwavering spirit. It's in the face of adversity that we find our voice, our purpose, and our unique gifts. The thing about love, yaar, is that it's not always sunshine and rainbows. It's a messy, complicated, and sometimes downright painful journey. But it's also a journey that can teach us so much about ourselves, about our strengths and weaknesses, about our deepest fears and desires.

It's like that one scene In Dil Chahta Hai, where Sid is heartbroken over Tara and goes on a solo trip to Goa. He mopes around, drinks beer, and listens to sad songs. But it's through this process of self-reflection and introspection that he finally comes to terms with his feelings and moves on.

Just like Sid, I had to go through my own version of Goa. It wasn't a physical journey, but an emotional one. It was a journey of self-discovery, of healing, and of learning to love myself again.

I realized that the key to moving on wasn't about forgetting the past, but about making peace with it. It was about accepting that things didn't work out with Rashmi, but that didn't mean I was any less worthy of love or happiness.

It was about understanding that love isn't a finite resource, that there's enough love in the world for everyone. It was about letting go of the anger, the resentment, and the bitterness, and replacing them with forgiveness, compassion, and gratitude.

And most importantly, it was about realizing that my happiness didn't depend on someone else's love, but on my own self-worth. It was about finding joy in the simple things, in pursuing my passions, in connecting with my friends and family.

So, yeah, love can be a bitch sometimes. It can leave you heartbroken, shattered, and feeling like you'll never find happiness again. But it can also be a catalyst for growth, a teacher that shows you the true meaning of resilience, self-love, and the power of letting go.

So, if you're going through a tough time, if you're feeling lost and alone, remember that you're not the only one. We've all been there, yaar. We've all felt the sting of heartbreak, the pain of rejection, the agony of unrequited love.

But remember, it's not the end. It's just a new beginning, a chance to rediscover yourself, to find your own path, and to create a life that is filled with joy, purpose, and love. Because just like those Bollywood movies, life has its own script, its own twists and turns. You might be playing the heartbroken hero right now, but trust me, there's a sequel waiting to be written, a sequel where you're the star of your own damn movie.

So, pick yourself up, dust yourself off, and get back in the game. Delete those old photos, unfollow those toxic exes, and start writing a new chapter. One filled with self-love, adventure, and maybe, just maybe, a new love that's even better than the last.

Remember, yaar, you're not just a player in this game of life; you're the director. You have the power to call the shots, to rewrite the script, and to create a happy ending that's worthy of a standing ovation. Don't let a Red Light hold you back. It's time to hit the gas and go for the Green Light, towards a future that's brighter, bolder, and full of possibilities.

But even as I tried to move on, the ghost of Rashmi lingered. One night, unable to resist the urge, I found myself scrolling through old WhatsApp chats, my heart aching with every message.

There it was, a string of unanswered "good mornings" and unreturned calls. Emoji hearts that once symbolized our love now felt like mocking reminders of my loneliness. One message in particular stuck out, a simple "I love you" sent a few days before she left. Her reply? A cold, curt "Seen."

That single word shattered me. It was like a final nail in the coffin of our relationship, a confirmation that she had moved on, leaving me behind to pick up the pieces of my broken heart. I sobbed uncontrollably, the weight of my grief crushing me like a tidal wave.

But as the tears subsided and the first rays of dawn peeked through my window, a strange calmness washed over me. A realization struck me, a thought that sent shivers down my spine.

"Today, I'm crying over a girl," I whispered to myself, "but one day, I'll be losing my life, my soul, my body. How will I face that day?"

The thought of my own mortality, the inevitability of death, put my heartbreak into perspective. Suddenly, my problems seemed trivial, my pain insignificant. What did it matter if Rashmi didn't love me back? What did it matter if I was heartbroken and alone? One day, it would all be over.

I switched off my phone, silencing the constant barrage of notifications, the reminders of a love that was no more. I took a deep breath, feeling a strange sense of peace wash over me. It was as if the fear of death had somehow liberated me from the shackles of my heartbreak.

That day, I took another step towards moving on. I didn't know what the future held, but I knew I wouldn't waste another precious moment on someone who didn't value me. I would focus on myself, my dreams, and my own happiness. After all, life is too short to dwell on what could have been. It's time to embrace the present, to live each day to the fullest, and to create a future that is worthy of the time we have left.

I knew I couldn't just sit around and wait for my wounds to heal. I had to take action, to proactively seek out the things that brought me joy and fulfillment.

So, I dusted off my old guitar, the one that had been gathering dust in the corner of my room for months. I started strumming chords, rediscovering the melodies that once filled my heart with warmth. I joined a local music group, jamming with fellow musicians and finding solace in the shared rhythm of our souls.

I also decided to get back into shape, not as a punishment for my emotional eating habits, but as a celebration of my body and its resilience. I hit the gym, pushing myself to new limits, feeling the endorphins course through my veins as I sweat out the toxins of heartbreak.

As I immersed myself in these activities, I started to feel a sense of purpose returning to my life. I realized that I had passions and interests beyond my failed relationship. I was more than just someone's ex; I was an individual with my own dreams, aspirations, and talents.

And slowly but surely, the pain began to subside. The memories of Rashmi didn't disappear completely, but they no longer held the same power over me. They became a part of my past, a chapter in my life that had shaped me, but not defined me.

I learned that moving on is not a linear process. It's a series of ups and downs, of good days and bad days. There were moments when I felt like I was taking two steps forward and one step back. But I persevered, reminding myself that progress, no matter how small, was still progress.

And then, one day, I woke up and realized that I hadn't thought about Rashmi in days. The thought of her no longer sent my heart racing or my mind spiraling. I had finally let go.

It wasn't a smooth ride, yaar. There were days when the memories flooded back, threatening to pull me under. But I had learned my lesson. I didn't let them consume me. I'd call a friend, hit the gym, or lose myself in a good book. I discovered that distraction wasn't just a way to avoid pain; it was a tool for healing, a way to create space for new experiences and new joys.

And slowly but surely, I began to rediscover myself. I wasn't just the guy who got his heart broken; I was a writer, a musician, a friend, a son, a brother. I had passions, dreams, and a whole life ahead of me. Rashmi was just a chapter, a significant one, but not the entire book.

So, yeah, love can be a bitch. It can knock you down, steal your breath, and leave you questioning everything. But it can also teach you valuable lessons, about yourself, about others, and about the unpredictable nature of life.

If you're going through a tough time, if you're feeling lost and alone, remember my story. Remember that even the darkest nights eventually give way to dawn. Remember that heartbreak is not the end, but a new beginning, a chance to rediscover yourself and create a life that is even more fulfilling than you ever imagined.

So, pick yourself up, dust yourself off, and take that first step towards healing. It won't be easy, but it's worth it. Because on the other side of heartbreak, there's a whole world waiting for you, a world full of love, laughter, and endless possibilities.

Remember, yaar, life is too short to dwell on the past. It's time to hit the Green Light and embrace the future, with all its uncertainties and exciting adventures. Who knows, your next chapter might just be your best one yet.

CHAPTER FOUR

TUG OF WAR WITH YOUR BRAIN

Life's a tug of war, yaar, a constant battle between the angel and devil sitting on your shoulders, whispering sweet nothings and tempting you with shortcuts. It's your brain, that jumbled mess of neurons and synapses, pulling you in opposite directions, one towards discipline and hard work, the other towards instant gratification and procrastination.

Remember that one time when Lalu Prasad Yadav, the king of political wit, was asked about his educational qualifications? He famously quipped, "I hold a degree from the University of Chapra." Now, for those not in the know, Chapra is not exactly an Ivy League institution. It's more like a school of hard knocks, where you learn the art of survival, street smarts, and how to charm your way out of any sticky situation.

Our brains are a bit like Lalu, yaar. They're a mix of brilliance and bumbling, of lofty aspirations and the occasional desire to just veg out and watch reruns of "Tarak

Mehta Ka Oolta Chashma."

One minute, you're all pumped up, ready to conquer the world, armed with a to-do list that could rival the Mahabharata. The next minute, you're sprawled on the couch, scrolling through Instagram reels of cute puppies and wondering if you can justify ordering pizza for the third time this week.

It's like your brain Is playing a game of tug of war with itself, and you're the rope, being pulled in opposite directions. One side is screaming, "Get up, you lazy bum! You've got goals to achieve, dreams to chase!" while the other side is whispering, "Just five more minutes of scrolling, then you can start that assignment...or maybe tomorrow."

And this internal tug of war, this constant push and pull between our aspirations and our distractions, is a universal struggle. Think of our netas, those politicians who promise us the moon during elections but end up getting caught in scams and scandals. Are they inherently evil, or are they simply succumbing to the temptations that come with power and fame?

It's like that one politician, caught red-handed accepting a suitcase full of cash. Maybe he started out with good intentions, wanting to serve the people. But somewhere along the way, the lure of easy money, the thrill of power, became too strong to resist. It's a classic case of the brain's tug of war, where the devil on his shoulder won out over the angel.

But it's not just politicians, yaar. We all face this internal battle every day. The student who knows he should be studying but can't resist the urge to scroll through social media. The entrepreneur who dreams of building a successful business but keeps getting sidetracked by the latest viral trends. The fitness enthusiast who vows to eat healthy but can't resist the lure of that cheesy pizza.

We're all guilty of it, right? We set goals, we make resolutions, but then our brains start playing tricks on us. They whisper excuses, they offer justifications, they tempt us with instant gratification. It's like a constant tug of war, and sometimes, it feels like we're losing.

But hey, don't worry, brother. We're not all doomed to become corrupt politicians or couch potatoes with a Netflix addiction. Just like those legendary cricketers who bounce back from a string of ducks to hit a century, we too can train our brains to win this tug of war.

It's all about building mental muscle. Just like you hit the gym to tone your biceps and triceps, you gotta exercise your brain to strengthen your willpower and focus. Think of it as a mental boot camp, where you push yourself to resist those tempting distractions and stay laser-focused on your goals.

And just like any good workout, it takes time, effort, and a whole lot of sweat (okay, maybe not actual sweat, but you get the point). You can't expect to go from zero to hero overnight. It's a gradual process, a series of small victories that build up to a major triumph.

But don't worry, you don't have to become a meditating monk or a productivity guru to win this battle. Start small, yaar. Set realistic goals, create a schedule, and stick to it (as much as possible, because let's be real, sometimes those Instagram reels are just too tempting to resist).

And when you do stumble, when that devil on your shoulder starts whispering sweet nothings in your ear, don't beat yourself up. Just pick yourself up, dust yourself off, and get back on track. Remember, even the greatest athletes have off days. The key is to learn from your mistakes, adjust your strategy, and keep moving forward.

Because just like our favorite Bollywood movies, life is full of second chances, dramatic comebacks, and unexpected plot twists. So, don't let your brain's tug of war hold you back. Train your mind, conquer your distractions, and become the hero of your own story.

And guess what ? This ain't just about willpower or some fancy meditation technique. It's about finding what works for you, what motivates you, what keeps you going when the going gets tough.

Maybe it's setting small, achievable goals, like our politicians do when they promise us "Acche Din" (good days) – one step at a time, building towards a brighter future. Maybe it's finding a workout buddy, someone who'll drag you to the gym even when you'd rather be binge-watching "Mirzapur." Or maybe it's rewarding yourself with a cheat meal (hello, butter chicken!) after a week of clean eating.

The key Is to find a system that works for you, one that keeps you motivated and on track. Remember, it's not about being perfect; it's about making progress.

So, embrace the chaos, bro. Embrace the quirks of your brain, the endless chatter, the constant tug of war between your aspirations and your distractions. It's what makes us human, what makes life interesting.

And hey, if all else fails, just remember the wise words of Rahul Gandhi: "This morning, I woke up at night." It might not make any sense, but it'll definitely make you laugh. And sometimes, laughter is the best way to win that tug of war with your brain.

So, learn laugh at yourself, Mere Bhai. Laugh at your mistakes, your imperfections, your weird and wonderful brain. And then, pick yourself up, dust yourself off, and keep moving forward. Because just like in those Bollywood movies, even the most chaotic of minds can create a masterpiece. It's all about finding the right rhythm, the right beat, and dancing to the tune of your own dhol.

But what's the dhol without a beat, right? You need a rhythm, a structure to keep you on track. And that's where willpower comes in. It's like the Amitabh Bachchan of your brain, the one who always gets the job done, no matter how tough the situation.

Now, willpower ain't some magical power that only superheroes possess. It's like a muscle, the more you use it, the stronger it gets. And just like pumping iron at the gym, building willpower takes practice and consistency.

One way to do this is by setting small, achievable goals, like our politicians do when they promise us "Acche Din" (good days) – one step at a time, building towards a brighter future. Start with small victories, like resisting that extra samosa or waking up fifteen minutes earlier. These small wins will fuel your confidence and strengthen your willpower muscle.

Another way to boost your willpower is by finding a workout buddy, someone who'll drag you to the gym even when you'd rather be binge-watching "Mirzapur." In the brain tug of war, having a support system is like having a whole team on your side, cheering you on and holding you accountable.

And don't forget the power of reward, yaar. After a week of slogging away at work or studies, treat yourself to a cheat meal or a night out with friends. It's like giving yourself a standing ovation after a stellar performance; it reinforces positive behavior and makes the journey more enjoyable.

But remember, moderation is key, my friend. Just like Gabbar Singh in Sholay, overindulging in those rewards can backfire. A cheat meal is fine, but a cheat week? That's a recipe for disaster, just like Gabbar's plan to loot Ramgarh.

Now, here's a secret weapon that even our politicians could learn from: self-compassion. It's like a warm hug from your mom after a bad day, a gentle reminder that it's okay to mess up sometimes.

Just like our cricket team can't win every match, you can't expect to win every battle against your brain. There will be days when you hit snooze one too many times, when you binge-watch Netflix instead of working on that project, when you reach for that bag of chips instead of the salad. And that's okay, yaar.

Don't beat yourself up over it. Instead, treat yourself with kindness and understanding, just like you would a friend. Acknowledge your slip-up, learn from it, and move on. Remember, even Rajinikanth has had a few flops in his career, but that didn't stop him from becoming the superstar he is today.

It's also important to remember that willpower isn't just about resisting temptation. It's also about harnessing your emotions and using them as fuel for your goals. Think of it like a Bollywood masala movie, where the hero's anger and passion ultimately lead him to victory.

Your emotions, just like those dramatic background scores in Bollywood movies, can either amplify your willpower or sabotage it. Learn to channel your frustration into motivation, your sadness into creativity, your anxiety into action.

And don't forget the power of visualization, yaar. Picture yourself achieving your goals, crossing that finish line, receiving that award, or simply living the life you've always dreamed of. Visualization is like a movie trailer for your life, giving you a glimpse of the awesome things that await you.

So, the next time you find yourself in a mental tug of war, remember these tips. Practice mindfulness, build your willpower muscle, embrace self-compassion, and use your emotions to your advantage.

And most importantly, don't forget to have fun along the way. Life's too short to be serious all the time, yaar. Dance to the beat of your own dhol, and remember, even in the midst of chaos, you can still create a masterpiece.

Remember, even Gabbar Singh had his moments of vulnerability, muttering "Kitne aadmi the?" in a rare display of fear. So, cut yourself some slack when your brain plays hooky. Acknowledge the slip-up, learn from it, and move on, just like Circuit bouncing back from his hilarious misadventures with Munna Bhai.

And just like Munna Bhai discovered the power of "jadoo ki jhappi" (the magical hug), find ways to comfort and encourage yourself when you stumble. Maybe it's treating yourself to a cup of chai and a plate of pakoras, watching a feel-good Bollywood flick, or simply talking to a friend who understands.

But hey, this ain't just about managing the mess, yaar. It's about using your brain's quirks to your advantage. Think of it like harnessing the power of a Jugaad – that uniquely Indian talent for finding creative solutions to everyday problems. Your brain, with its seemingly chaotic wiring and unpredictable impulses, is actually a treasure trove of creativity and innovation.

Just like those Bollywood heroes who turn their weaknesses into strengths, you too can leverage your brain's tug of war to achieve your dreams. Embrace the chaos, channel your emotions, and use your unique blend of logic and intuition to navigate the challenges of life.

So, the next time you find your brain playing tug of war, don't despair. Remember, you're not alone in this struggle. We all have our inner Lalu Prasad Yadav moments, but we also have the potential to be the Rajinikanth of our own lives.

And if all else fails, just remember the wise words of Rancho from "3 Idiots": "Aal izz well!" After all, even in the midst of a chaotic tug of war, there's always a chance for a happy ending.

Picture this, yaar: you're standing at the edge of a cliff, the wind whipping through your hair, the vast expanse of the ocean stretching out before you. It's a scene straight out of a Yash Chopra movie, filled with drama, longing, and a touch of melancholy.

But this ain't just any cliff, my friend. This is the precipice of your dreams, the point where you decide whether to take a leap of faith or stay rooted in the safety of the familiar. It's a moment of truth, a test of your courage and conviction.

And just like those Bollywood heroes who face their inner demons before conquering the world, you too must confront the doubts and fears that hold you back. You must silence the naysayers, both inside and outside your head, and embrace the uncertainty of the unknown.

It's not easy, yaar. It's scary as hell. The fear of failure, the fear of rejection, the fear of the unknown can paralyze you, like a deer caught in the headlights of an oncoming truck.

But remember, even Shah Rukh Khan started out as a struggling actor, facing countless rejections before becoming the King of Bollywood. He took that leap of faith, embraced his vulnerabilities, and emerged stronger and more determined than ever.

So, what's stopping you, my friend? What's holding you back from taking that first step, from chasing your dreams, from living a life that makes your heart sing?

Is it the fear of failure? Remember, failure is not the opposite of success; it's a part of it. It's a stepping stone, a learning experience, a chance to pick yourself up and try again.

Is it the fear of rejection? Remember, not everyone will understand or support your dreams, and that's okay. What matters is that you believe in yourself, that you have the courage to stand up for what you want, even if it means facing a few naysayers along the way.

Or is it the fear of the unknown? Remember, the most exciting adventures often lie beyond our comfort zones. It's in the uncharted territories, the unexplored paths, that we discover our true potential and create a life that's truly our own.

So, what if that cliff isn't just a metaphor, yaar? What if it's the very real fear of uncertainty that's holding you back? The "kya hoga" (what if) syndrome that plagues us all, the nagging doubt that whispers, "What if I fail? What if I make the wrong choice? What if I regret it later?"

It's like that scene in "Dilwale Dulhania Le Jayenge" where Simran stands at the train station, torn between her love for Raj and her duty to her family. It's a heart-wrenching moment, a battle between the known and the unknown, between the safe path and the one that leads to her true happiness.

We've all been there, yaar. We've all stood at that crossroads, unsure of which path to take, paralyzed by the fear of what lies ahead. We cling to the familiar, even if it's not what we truly want, because it's safe, it's predictable, it's comfortable.

But what if, just like Simran, we gathered the courage to take that leap of faith? What if we embraced the uncertainty, the not knowing, and trusted that whatever happens, we'll find a way to make it work?

It's like jumping into the deep end of the pool without knowing how to swim. It's terrifying, exhilarating, and ultimately, liberating. Because once you let go of the fear of uncertainty, you open yourself up to a world of possibilities. You free yourself from the shackles of doubt and self-limitation, and you step into a life that's truly yours.

And just like those iconic Bollywood songs that capture the bittersweet pain and joy of love, uncertainty can be a source of both anxiety and excitement. It's the thrill of the chase, the anticipation of the unknown, the hope for a better tomorrow.

So, embrace the uncertainty, yaar. Let it fuel your passion, ignite your creativity, and propel you towards your dreams. Remember, even the most successful people in the world started out with nothing but a dream and a willingness to take a risk.

Just like those Bollywood underdogs who defy the odds and emerge victorious, you too can overcome your fear of uncertainty and create a life that's truly extraordinary.

Think about it, yaar. Life throws curveballs faster than a Kapil Dev outswinger. One moment you're cruising along, singing "Aaj main upar, aasman niche," feeling on top of the world. The next, you're facing a setback that leaves you feeling like you've been hit by a Mumbai local train during rush hour.

It's like that time your crush rejected you, leaving you with a heartbreak heavier than a Sabyasachi lehenga. Or that time you missed a crucial deadline at work, feeling the heat from your boss hotter than a Rajasthan summer.

These unexpected turns can leave you feeling lost, confused, and questioning everything you thought you knew. It's like trying to navigate a Delhi traffic jam without a GPS – you know where you want to go, but the path ahead seems blocked at every turn.

This is where the real tug of war begins, the one between your hopes and fears, your dreams and doubts. It's a battle that takes place not on a physical rope, but in the depths of your soul.

One side of you screams, "Don't give up! You've got this! Remember all the times you've overcome challenges in the past?" It's the voice of your inner warrior, the one who refuses to let setbacks define you.

But the other side whispers, "What's the point? It's too hard. You're not good enough. Why even bother trying?" It's the voice of your inner critic, the one who feeds on your insecurities and doubts.

It's a constant push and pull, a relentless battle for dominance. And the outcome, my friend, depends on which side you choose to listen to.

Do you listen to the voice of fear and doubt, allowing it to paralyze you and keep you stuck in a rut? Or do you listen to the voice of courage and hope, the one that urges you to rise above the challenges and create the life you desire?

It's a choice, yaar, a choice that only you can make. And just like those epic Mahabharata battles where the fate of entire kingdoms hung in the balance, the outcome of this tug of war will determine the course of your life.

Imagine this, brother: you're standing at the edge of a bustling marketplace, the air thick with the aroma of spices and sweets. It's a scene straight out of Chandni Chowk,

Delhi, filled with vibrant colors, a cacophony of sounds, and a dizzying array of choices.

But this isn't just any marketplace, my friend. This is the bazaar of life, where you're bombarded with endless options and opportunities. It's a place where dreams are made and broken, where fortunes are won and lost, where the future seems as unpredictable as the monsoon rains.

And just like those shoppers who wander through the market, wide-eyed and overwhelmed, we too can feel lost and confused when faced with uncertainty. The fear of making the wrong choice, the pressure to keep up with others, the nagging doubt that whispers, "What if I miss out on something better?"

It's like standing in front of a chaat stall, unsure whether to order the gol gappe, the aloo tikki, or the papdi chaat. Each option seems tempting, but you're afraid of missing out on the taste of the others.

But remember, yaar, life isn't about always making the perfect choice. It's about experiencing the journey, savoring the flavors, and learning from the missteps. Just like that time you accidentally ordered the extra spicy pani puri and ended up with a runny nose and teary eyes, you might encounter unexpected twists and turns along the way.

But that's okay, my friend. It's all part of the adventure. It's about embracing the uncertainty, taking risks, and discovering what truly makes your taste buds tingle, what truly makes your heart sing.

So, the next time you feel lost and overwhelmed by the choices before you, take a deep breath and remember those crowded marketplaces where chaos and excitement coexist. Channel your inner Jugaadu, and find creative solutions to the challenges you face. Embrace the unexpected, trust your instincts, and remember that sometimes, the most delicious surprises come from taking a chance on something new.

Remember, even the most experienced chefs started by burning a few rotis or over-salting the dal. It's through those culinary mishaps that they learned, grew, and ultimately created dishes that make our taste buds dance with joy.

Similarly, your journey through life's marketplace is filled with trial and error, with unexpected detours and surprising discoveries. It's about learning to navigate the chaos, to trust your gut feeling, and to embrace the unknown with a sense of curiosity and wonder.

So, the next time you feel that knot of uncertainty tightening in your stomach, remember those bustling marketplaces where chaos and excitement coexist. Channel your inner Jugaadu, and find creative solutions to the challenges you face. Embrace the unexpected, trust your instincts, and remember that sometimes, the most delicious surprises come from taking a chance on something new.

But hey, this isn't just about navigating the external chaos, yaar. It's about finding peace amidst the internal turmoil, that constant chatter in your head that can sometimes feel like a Mumbai fish market at peak hour.

It's about creating a sense of calm amidst the storm, like a serene oasis in the middle of a bustling city. It's about learning to silence the doubts and fears that hold you back, and embracing the quiet confidence that comes from knowing you're capable of handling whatever life throws your way.

Think of it like finding a peaceful corner in a crowded railway station, where you can close your eyes, take a deep breath, and simply be. It's about finding that inner sanctuary where you can recharge, refocus, and reconnect with your true self.

And just like those moments of stillness in a bustling city, finding inner peace amidst the chaos of life requires practice and patience. It's about learning to meditate, to focus on your breath, to let go of the worries that weigh you down.

It's about finding solace in the simple things, like a cup of steaming masala chai on a rainy day, the comforting melody of a Kishore Kumar song, or a heartfelt conversation with a loved one under a starry sky.

Just like those Bollywood movies that always have a song for every emotion, life too offers us moments of respite, of tranquility, of inner peace. It's about finding those moments, cherishing them, and using them to recharge our batteries.

But hey, this ain't just about sitting around and meditating all day, yaar. It's about finding a balance, a rhythm that works for you. Just like a Bollywood dance sequence, life is a mix of fast-paced action, soulful melodies, and moments of quiet reflection.

So, find your rhythm, my friend. Find the beat that resonates with your soul, the melody that makes your heart sing. Embrace the chaos, cherish the calm, and remember that even in the midst of uncertainty, there's always a chance to dance to the tune of your own dhol.

And just like those iconic Bollywood dialogues that stay with us long after the movie ends, here's a mantra for you to carry with you: "Don't be afraid to fall, yaar. Just remember, even the stars stumble sometimes. But they always find a way to shine brighter."

So, let the chaos of life be your dance floor, my friend. Let the uncertainty be your music. And remember, you are the choreographer of your own destiny, the master of your own fate.

You have the power to turn your struggles into strengths, your doubts into decisions, your fears into fuel for your dreams. Just like those Bollywood heroes who rise above their circumstances and find their happily ever after, you too can create a life that's filled with joy, purpose, and fulfillment.

So, let go of the fear, embrace the unknown, and trust in the journey. Because even amidst the chaos, there's a beautiful symphony waiting to be discovered.

And remember, yaar, even if life throws you a curveball, even if you stumble and fall, even if you feel lost and confused, never forget that you are capable of so much more than you think.

You are a force to be reckoned with, a star waiting to shine, a hero in the making.

Now go out there and conquer the world, one step at a time.

Because remember, in the grand Bollywood movie of your life, the ending is yet to be written. And it's up to you to make it a blockbuster.

CHAPTER FIVE

MARBLES OF SELF LOVE

Picture this, first: It's a sweltering summer afternoon in the heart of Chandni Chowk, Delhi. The air is thick with the aroma of kebabs sizzling on skewers and the sweet scent of jalebis frying in hot oil. A young boy, barely ten years old, sits hunched over a wooden cart, his eyes glued to a worn-out comic book. He's oblivious to the chaos around him, the honking of cars, the chatter of haggling shoppers, the cries of street vendors hawking their wares.

His name is Chintu, and he's a dreamer. He dreams of becoming a superhero, of flying through the air and rescuing damsels in distress. But for now, he's content to escape into the world of comics, where anything is possible.

As he flips through the pages, his eyes light up as he comes across a story about a young boy who discovers he has superpowers. The boy can fly, lift heavy objects, and even become invisible. Chintu's heart races with excitement. Could he too have hidden powers? Could he be destined for greatness?

But just as quickly as the excitement arises, it's replaced by a wave of self-doubt. He looks down at his skinny arms, his worn-out clothes, his ordinary surroundings. How could someone like him ever be a superhero?

This, my friend, is the tug of war of self-love. It's the battle between the Chintu inside all of us, the one who dreams big and believes in the impossible, and the inner critic who whispers, "You're not good enough, you're not special, you'll never amount to anything."

It's a battle that takes place in the quiet corners of our minds, in the moments of self-reflection, in the mirror we face every morning. It's a battle that can either empower us or cripple us, depending on which side wins.

But here's the thing, yaar: the Chintu inside all of us is right. We are capable of extraordinary things. We all have hidden talents, unique strengths, and the potential to make a difference in the world.

Just like Chintu's comic book hero, we all have our own superpowers. It might not be the ability to fly or become invisible, but it's something equally valuable. It might be your creativity, your resilience, your empathy, your sense of humor. It might be your ability to connect with people, to inspire others, to bring joy and laughter into the world.

But just like Chintu, we often doubt our own abilities. We let our inner critic convince us that we're not good enough, that we're not worthy of love and success. We compare ourselves to others, forgetting that we are all unique individuals with our own special gifts to offer.

It's like that scene in "3 Idiots" where Rancho encourages his friends to pursue their passions, to follow their hearts, to "chase excellence, and success will follow." It's a powerful message, a reminder that we should never let anyone tell us what we can or cannot do.

But sometimes, we need a little push, a little encouragement, to believe in ourselves. We need someone to tell us, "You've got this, yaar! You're amazing, you're capable, you're worthy of love and happiness."

And sometimes, that encouragement comes from the most unexpected places. Like that old uncle at a family wedding who tells you, "Beta, you have a spark in your eyes. Don't let anyone dim it." Or that auto-rickshaw driver who shares his life story with you, reminding you that everyone has struggles, but it's our spirit that truly matters.

These are the marbles of self-love, yaar. They're not about arrogance or vanity, but about recognizing your worth, embracing your flaws, and celebrating your uniqueness. It's about looking in the mirror and saying, "I am enough. I am worthy of love, happiness, and success."

But just like those intricate rangoli patterns that take time and patience to create, self-love isn't built overnight. It's a journey, a process of self-discovery, of learning to appreciate the beauty and complexity of your own being.

It's about silencing that inner critic, that nagging voice that tells you you're not good enough. It's about replacing those negative thoughts with positive affirmations, like "I am strong, I am capable, I am worthy."

It's about surrounding yourself with people who lift you up, who believe in you, who see the best in you. It's about letting go of toxic relationships, those that drain your energy and make you doubt yourself.

And most importantly, it's about treating yourself with kindness and compassion, just like you would a friend. It's about forgiving yourself for your mistakes, acknowledging your vulnerabilities, and embracing your imperfections.

It's about looking at yourself in the mirror, not with the critical eye of a fashion police inspector judging your outfit, but with the loving gaze of a parent admiring their child. It's about seeing the beauty in your flaws, the strength in your vulnerability, the resilience in your spirit.

Remember, yaar, you're not just a collection of likes and comments on social media. You're not just a number on a weighing scale or a grade on a report card. You're a unique individual with a story to tell, a song to sing, a dance to perform.

So, embrace your quirks, your passions, your dreams. Wear your heart on your sleeve, even if it means getting a little messy sometimes. Dance like no one's watching, sing like no one's listening, and love yourself unconditionally, just like your mom does.

And just like those Bollywood movies that teach us the importance of family, remember that you're not alone in this journey of self-love. You have a tribe of friends, family, and loved ones who cherish you for who you are, flaws and all.

So, reach out to them, lean on them, let them shower you with their love and support. And most importantly, be kind to yourself, yaar. Because you deserve all the love, happiness, and success that life has to offer.

Remember, self-love isn't a destination, it's a journey. It's a lifelong process of learning, growing, and evolving. It's about embracing the good, the bad, and the ugly, and recognizing that all of it makes you who you are.

So, take a deep breath, look in the mirror, and say to yourself, "I am worthy. I am enough. I am loved." Because, my friend, that's the truth. And the sooner you believe it, the sooner you'll start living a life that's truly yours.

Life, just like a game of cricket, throws us googlies and bouncers. Sometimes, we hit them out of the park, and sometimes, we get clean bowled. But it's not the number of runs you score or the wickets you take that define you. It's your ability to dust yourself off, pick up the bat again, and face the next ball with renewed determination.

The same goes for the game of self-love. It's not about being perfect all the time. It's about acknowledging your mistakes, learning from them, and forgiving yourself. It's about being your own cheerleader, even when you feel like the whole world is booing you.

Think of it like a Bollywood movie, where the hero always has a few setbacks before he finally triumphs over the villain. There might be misunderstandings, heartbreaks, even a few slapstick comedy moments. But in the end, he always manages to pick himself up, overcome the odds, and win the day.

That's how you need to approach the game of self-love, yaar. When you stumble, when you make a mistake, when you feel like you've let yourself down, don't give up. Instead, take a deep breath, channel your inner Rajinikanth, and say, "Enna Rascala!"

Remember, every setback is an opportunity for growth. Every mistake is a lesson learned. Every challenge is a chance to prove to yourself how strong and resilient you truly are.

So, don't be afraid to fall, my friend. Don't be afraid to make mistakes. Don't be afraid to show your vulnerability. Embrace the imperfections, the quirks, the messy bits of your soul. Because that's what makes you human, that's what makes you beautiful.

And just like those iconic Bollywood characters who have taught us the true meaning of self-love, you too can learn to embrace your flaws and imperfections.

Remember Geet from "Jab We Met," who taught us to love ourselves unconditionally, to dance to the beat of our own drum, and to never apologize for being ourselves? Or Munna Bhai, who showed us that even the most flawed individuals can make a difference in the world with their unique brand of love and compassion?

These characters remind us that self-love isn't about being perfect, it's about being authentic. It's about accepting who we are, with all our quirks and idiosyncrasies. It's about loving ourselves, not in spite of our flaws, but because of them.

So, the next time you catch yourself playing the comparison game, scrolling through Instagram and feeling envious of others, remember that you are enough. You are worthy of love and happiness, just as you are.

Stop trying to fit into someone else's mold, yaar. Break free from the shackles of societal expectations and embrace your individuality. Be the quirky, imperfect, perfectly imperfect version of yourself.

Just like those Bollywood heroes who find love in the most unexpected places, self-love too can be found in the most unexpected corners of your heart. It might be hidden behind a wall of self-doubt, buried under layers of past hurt, or masked by a façade of bravado.

But it's there, yaar. It's waiting to be discovered, to be nurtured, to be unleashed. And once you find it, you'll realize that it's the most valuable marble you'll ever own.

Think about it like this: Imagine a young woman named Priya, working in a bustling Mumbai call center. She's got the gift of gab, a voice that could charm a snake out of its basket, and a knack for resolving customer complaints with a smile. But deep down, she feels like a fraud. She sees her colleagues climbing the corporate ladder, getting promotions and accolades, while she remains stuck in the same position.

Her inner critic whispers, "You're not smart enough, you're not ambitious enough, you'll never be anything more than a call center operator." She starts to believe these lies, her self-confidence dwindling like a mobile phone battery on a long train journey.

But one day, Priya stumbles upon a self-help book that talks about the importance of self-love. It's like a ray of sunshine breaking through the monsoon clouds, illuminating a path she hadn't considered before.

She starts practicing self-compassion, forgiving herself for past mistakes and acknowledging her strengths. She starts setting small goals for herself, like learning a new language or taking a dance class. And slowly but surely, she starts to see herself in a new light.

She realizes that her ability to connect with people, her empathy, and her communication skills are valuable assets, not just in her job, but in life. She starts to appreciate her quirky sense of humor, her love for Bollywood gossip, and her passion for street food.

And as she starts to embrace her unique qualities, her confidence grows. She starts taking on new challenges at work, volunteering for projects that push her out of her comfort zone. And guess what? She starts getting noticed. Her bosses see her potential, her colleagues admire her spirit, and she finally gets that promotion she's been dreaming of.

But the real victory, yaar, isn't the promotion or the recognition. It's the newfound love and respect she has for herself. It's the realization that she's not just a call center operator, she's a smart, capable, and worthy individual with a bright future ahead of her.

This is your story, yaar. It's a Bollywood blockbuster waiting to happen, a tale of self-discovery, of overcoming obstacles, of finding love in the most unexpected places – even within yourself. It's a story that deserves to be told, a story that will inspire others, a story that will make you proud. There will be moments of doubt, of setbacks, of feeling like you're taking two steps back for every step forward.

But that's okay, yaar. It's all part of the process. It's like a Bollywood dance sequence, where the choreography gets more complex and challenging as the song progresses. You might stumble, you might miss a step, but as long as you keep dancing, as long as you keep moving forward, you'll eventually find your rhythm.

And just like those Bollywood heroes who always have a catchy song for every situation, you too can create your own soundtrack for self-love. It might be a playlist of upbeat bhangra songs that get you pumped up, or soulful melodies that soothe your soul. It might be a collection of motivational quotes that remind you of your worth, or a journal filled with your hopes and dreams.

Whatever it is, find something that resonates with you, something that helps you connect with your inner self, something that reminds you of your own unique melody.

So, the next time you feel like you're losing at the game of self-love, remember Chintu, the boy who dreamed of becoming a superhero. Remember Priya, the call center operator who discovered her hidden talents. Remember all those Bollywood characters who taught us the true meaning of self-acceptance and self-worth.

And most importantly, remember that you are not alone. You have a whole community of friends, family, and loved ones who are cheering you on, who believe in you, who love you for who you are.

So, take a deep breath, yaar, and let go of those self-limiting beliefs. You are not defined by your past mistakes, your perceived failures, or the opinions of others. You are a work in progress, a masterpiece in the making, a shining star waiting to be discovered.

So, start collecting those marbles of self-love. Fill your bag with kindness, compassion, and acceptance. Celebrate your victories, learn from your mistakes, and never stop believing in yourself.

Remember, you are not just a player in this game of life. You are the hero, the champion, the one who gets to write their own ending.

Remember, self-love isn't a one-time deal, yaar. It's a daily practice, a conscious effort to choose yourself, to prioritize your well-being, to be your own biggest fan. It's about looking in the mirror each morning and saying, "I hear you, and I love you."

So, let's raise a toast to self-love, shall we? Let's celebrate the quirks, the flaws, the imperfections that make us who we are. Let's embrace our inner Chintu and unleash our superpowers. Let's dance to the beat of our own dhol and write our own blockbusters.

Because, my friend, you are worthy of love, happiness, and success. You are the hero of your own story, the author of your own destiny. So go out there and create a life that makes you proud, a life that makes your heart sing, a life that's truly yours.

And remember, when life gets tough, when the self-doubt creeps in, when the world seems to be against you, just repeat after me: "Main apna favorite hoon!" (I am my own favorite!).

Because, yaar, that's the ultimate truth. And the sooner you embrace it, the sooner you'll start living a life that's truly extraordinary.

Even the mighty Akbar, the emperor who ruled over a vast empire, wasn't immune to self-doubt. Imagine him pacing the opulent halls of his palace, his mind a whirlwind of questions and concerns. "Was that policy decision truly wise? Did I choose the right path for my kingdom? Will my legacy be one of greatness or folly?"

In those moments of uncertainty, he didn't turn to his courtiers or advisors. Instead, he sought the company of Birbal, his trusted confidant and court jester. Birbal, with his sharp wit and clever wordplay, had a knack for putting things in perspective.

Think of it like that time Birbal asked Akbar to find the most foolish person in the kingdom. Akbar scoured his empire, only to present a man who had sold his house to buy a talking parrot. Birbal, with a sly smile, pointed out that Akbar himself was the most foolish, for he had given away a kingdom's worth of wisdom for a mere bird.

Just like Akbar, we all need a Birbal in our lives – a friend, a mentor, or a loved one who can offer us a fresh perspective, a dose of humor, and a gentle nudge in the right direction when self-doubt creeps in. They remind us of our strengths, help us laugh at our follies, and encourage us to keep moving forward, even when the path ahead seems uncertain.

So, the next time you find yourself doubting your own worth or second-guessing your decisions, remember Akbar and Birbal. Remember that even the greatest emperors had their moments of insecurity, but they didn't let those doubts define them. They sought wisdom, they embraced laughter, and they continued to lead with confidence and compassion.

And just like Akbar, you too have the power to overcome your self-doubt and embrace your own unique brand of greatness. So, find your Birbal, yaar, and let them help you navigate the ups and downs of life with a smile on your face and a song in your heart.

But even with a Birbal by our side, we'll still face moments when that inner critic starts to rear its ugly head. It might show up as a nagging voice in our head, questioning our every move, or as a persistent feeling of inadequacy, comparing ourselves to others and finding ourselves lacking.

Think of it like those pesky mosquitoes that buzz around your ears on a summer night, disrupting your sleep and leaving you feeling irritated and frustrated. Those negative thoughts and self-doubts can be just as annoying, just as persistent, and just as capable of draining your energy and joy.

But just as you wouldn't let a few mosquitoes ruin your sleep, you shouldn't let your inner critic dictate your self-worth. It's time to swat those negative thoughts away, yaar, and reclaim your power.

So, how do you do it? Well, it's not about denying those negative thoughts or pretending they don't exist. It's about acknowledging them, recognizing their presence, and then choosing not to engage with them.

It's like that time when you accidentally spilled chai on your favorite kurta. You could have spent the whole day cursing yourself, feeling embarrassed and frustrated. But instead, you took a deep breath, cleaned up the mess, and moved on.

Similarly, when those negative thoughts arise, don't get caught up in them. Observe them, acknowledge their presence, and then gently let them go. It's like watching a cloud pass by in the sky. You don't try to stop it or control it; you simply observe it and let it float away.

But sometimes, those negative thoughts can be persistent, like a stubborn stain that refuses to budge. In those moments, you need a stronger weapon, a more powerful tool to fight back. And that weapon, my friend, is self-compassion.

Think of self-compassion as a warm cup of chai on a chilly winter morning, a soothing balm for your weary soul. It's about treating yourself with the same kindness and understanding that you would offer to a friend in need. It's about recognizing that you're not perfect, that you're allowed to make mistakes, that you're worthy of love and forgiveness, even when you stumble and fall.

Just like our mothers, who always seem to have a comforting word or a warm embrace ready for us, no matter what we've done, we too need to cultivate that same unconditional love and acceptance towards ourselves.

It's not about being self-indulgent or making excuses for our shortcomings. It's about recognizing that we are all human, that we all have our struggles, and that we all deserve to be treated with kindness and respect, especially by ourselves.

So, the next time that inner critic starts whispering doubts and criticisms in your ear, try to counter it with a dose of self-compassion. Remind yourself of all the things you've accomplished, the challenges you've overcome, the kindness you've shown to others.

Remember those times when you helped a friend in need, or volunteered your time for a worthy cause, or simply made someone laugh with your silly jokes. These are the marbles of self-love that you've already collected, the proof that you are a good person, a kind person, a person worthy of love and respect.

And just like those precious marbles that you wouldn't dream of throwing away, hold onto those memories, those moments of kindness, those acts of selflessness. They are a testament to your character, a reminder of your worth, a source of strength and inspiration.

So, embrace your inner Munna Bhai, yaar. Cultivate that same childlike wonder, that infectious enthusiasm, that unwavering belief in the power of love and forgiveness. And most importantly, be kind to yourself.

Because just as every story needs a supporting cast, your self-love journey needs a cheering squad. Surround yourself with friends and family who celebrate your victories, comfort you during your setbacks, and remind you of your worth when you forget.

Think of those scenes in "Dil Chahta Hai" where three friends support each other through thick and thin, or the emotional bond between the brothers in "Josh." These portrayals of friendship remind us of the power of human connection, the importance of having people in our lives who lift us up and believe in us, even when we don't believe in ourselves.

Just like those friends who always have your back, your support system can help you navigate the ups and downs of life. They can offer a listening ear, a shoulder to cry on, or a much-needed pep talk when you're feeling down. They can remind you of your strengths, your accomplishments, and your potential, even when you can't see it yourself.

So, don't be afraid to lean on your loved ones, yaar. Don't be ashamed to ask for help when you need it. Remember, even superheroes need sidekicks sometimes.

But self-love isn't just about external validation. It's also about cultivating a positive internal dialogue, a voice within yourself that speaks with kindness, compassion, and encouragement.

This mantra of self-belief and manifestation can be a powerful tool in your arsenal of self-love. By repeating positive affirmations, by visualizing your goals, by constantly reminding yourself of your worth, you can start to rewire your brain and create a more positive self-image.

But just like those Bollywood movies that have a few twists and turns before the happy ending, your journey of self-love won't always be smooth sailing. There will be moments of doubt, of setbacks, of feeling like you're taking two steps back for every step forward. Just ask our friend, Raju Rastogi from "3 Idiots." Remember how he struggled with crippling anxiety and fear of failure, constantly comparing himself to his overachieving friends? He was trapped in a cycle of self-doubt, convinced that he wasn't good enough, smart enough, or lucky enough to succeed. But, like a true Bollywood hero, Raju eventually found his own path, his own unique way of shining. He realized that success isn't just about topping exams or landing a high-paying job. It's about finding your passion, following your dreams, and living a life that's true to yourself.

So, even when those negative thoughts creep in, whispering doubts and criticisms in your ear, remember Raju's transformation. Remember that you are not defined by your failures, your setbacks, or the opinions of others. You are a unique individual with your own strengths, talents, and aspirations.

Just like Raju, you have the power to break free from the chains of self-doubt and embrace your own path to happiness. And remember, sometimes the most fulfilling journeys are the ones that take unexpected detours and lead us to discover hidden treasures within ourselves.

So, the next time you feel like you're losing at the game of self-love, take a deep breath and remember Raju's journey. Remind yourself that you are capable, you are worthy, and you have the power to create your own happy ending.

And just like Circuit, who despite his hilarious antics, showed unwavering loyalty and love for Munna Bhai, remember that you have people in your life who cherish you for who you are, quirks and all. They see your value, your potential, and your unique spark. Let their love and support be a guiding light in your journey of self-love.

So, let's make a pact. Let's promise to be kind to ourselves, to forgive our mistakes, to celebrate our victories, no matter how small. Let's silence that inner critic and embrace our inner rockstar.

Remember, the game of marbles of self-love is not about winning or losing. It's about playing with an open heart, embracing the ups and downs, and learning to love yourself unconditionally. Because when you truly love yourself, you'll find that you have the power to achieve anything you set your mind to.

So, go on, yaar. Pick up those marbles, dust them off, and start playing. It's your game, your rules, your life. Make it a masterpiece!

CHAPTER SIX

SQUID GAME OF SOCIAL MEDIA

Where Likes Are the New Currency and FOMO Is the Real Monster

Picture this, Bro: Your phone buzzes with a notification. It's Rahul, your college buddy, posting a selfie from his Goa vacation. He's lounging on a beach, sipping a coconut, with a caption that reads, "Living my best life!" You glance at your own reflection in the laptop screen, bleary-eyed from a late-night work session, with a half-eaten bowl of Maggi noodles as your only companion. Suddenly, a wave of FOMO (Fear of Missing Out) washes over you, leaving you feeling like you're stuck in the "Red Light, Green Light" game of life while everyone else is dancing to "Badtameez Dil" on a Goan beach.

Welcome to the Squid Game of Social Media, my friend, where likes are the new currency, followers are your army, and FOMO is the real monster lurking in the shadows. It's a game where everyone seems to be living their best life, while you're stuck scrolling through endless reels of perfectly curated vacations, aesthetically pleasing food pics, and inspirational quotes that make you question your own life choices.

But hey, don't worry, yaar. We've all been there. We've all fallen prey to the seductive allure of social media, the endless scroll that promises entertainment, connection, and a glimpse into the lives of others.

Remember that time Rahul posted a picture of himself bungee jumping in New Zealand? It was like a scene straight out of "Zindagi Na Milegi Dobara," except instead of feeling inspired, you felt a pang of envy. You started questioning your own life choices, wondering why you weren't as adventurous, as spontaneous, as "cool" as Rahul.

But what you didn't see, my friend, was the behind-the-scenes footage. You didn't see Rahul throwing up after the jump, or the hours he spent agonizing over which filter to use for his Instagram post. You only saw the carefully curated highlight reel, the version of his life that he wanted to project to the world.

And that's the problem with social media, yaar. It's like a movie trailer, showing you only the most exciting, glamorous, and picture-perfect moments. It's easy to forget that real life, just like a Bollywood movie, has its fair share of drama, heartache, and even a few slapstick comedy scenes.

So, how do you navigate this Squid Game of Social Media, where the lines between reality and fantasy blur faster than a shape-shifting villain in a Rohit Shetty film? Well, the first step is to realize that you're not alone in this struggle. We all get caught up in the comparison game, the endless pursuit of likes and validation.

Remember those times when you meticulously crafted a witty tweet, only to receive a handful of likes? Or when you posted a picture of your delicious homemade biryani, only to be overshadowed by Rahul's perfectly plated avocado toast? It's enough to make you want to throw your phone out the window and move to a remote Himalayan village with no Wi-Fi.

But here's the thing, yaar: social media is a highlight reel, not a real-life reel. It's a curated version of reality, a carefully constructed façade that often hides the struggles, insecurities, and everyday challenges that we all face.

So, the next time you find yourself scrolling through your feed, feeling like you're missing out on all the fun, take a deep breath and remind yourself that social media is not a reflection of real life. It's a filtered, edited, and often exaggerated version of reality.

Just like those stories that have a happy ending, we often forget that the characters go through a lot of drama and heartache before they reach their happily ever after. Similarly, the people you see on social media may be struggling with their own demons, even if their posts suggest otherwise.

So, don't let the FOMO monster get to you, yaar. Don't let social media dictate your self-worth or make you feel like you're not good enough. Remember, you're living your own unique story, your own Bollywood blockbuster, and it's not about competing with others, it's about being the best version of yourself.

But hey, this doesn't mean you have to delete all your social media accounts and become a digital hermit. It just means being mindful of how you use it and not letting it consume your life.

Think of it like enjoying a plate of gol gappas at a street food stall. You savor the flavors, you enjoy the experience, but you don't let it become your entire diet. Similarly, you can use social media to connect with friends, share your experiences, and stay informed, but don't let it become your sole source of entertainment or validation.

So, what's the game plan, you ask? How do you win this Squid Game of Social Media without losing your sanity or becoming a digital hermit? Well, yaar, it's all about finding the right strategy, the right balance that works for you.

First up, we've got the "Marie Kondo" approach. Remember that Japanese organizing guru who taught us to declutter our homes by asking if an item sparks joy? Well, it's time to apply that same principle to your social media feed.

Take a good hard look at the accounts you follow, the pages you like, the groups you're a part of. Do they spark joy? Do they uplift you, inspire you, make you laugh? Or do they leave you feeling inadequate, envious, or downright depressed?

If it's the latter, then it's time to hit the "unfollow" button faster than you can say "nice pic." Declutter your digital life, yaar, and surround yourself with content that genuinely makes you happy. Follow those meme pages that make you laugh out loud, those inspirational accounts that motivate you to be a better version of yourself, those food bloggers who make you drool over their culinary creations.

But remember, just like decluttering your wardrobe, this isn't a one-time thing. It's an ongoing process. You need to regularly check in with yourself and ask if your social media feed is still serving you, or if it's time for another round of digital spring cleaning.

Next up, we've got the "Digital Detox" challenge. It's like taking a break from the hustle and bustle of city life and escaping to the serene mountains or the tranquil countryside. Just like our bodies need rest and rejuvenation, our minds too need a break from the constant stimulation of social media.

So, set aside some time each day, or even a whole day each week, to disconnect from the digital world. Switch off your phone, put away your laptop, and engage in activities that nourish your soul. Read a book, go for a walk, spend time with loved ones, or simply do nothing and let your mind wander.

Think of it like a meditation retreat, where you disconnect from the outside world and reconnect with your inner self. It's a chance to recharge your batteries, to clear your head, and to gain a fresh perspective on life.

But hey, this doesn't mean you have to go off the grid completely. You can still enjoy the benefits of social media without letting it take over your life. It's all about finding the right balance, the right amount of screen time that works for you.

Just like you go to theater tp watch movies that have an interval, where you can grab a samosa and catch your breath before the second half, you too can take regular breaks from social media to refresh and recharge.

And if you're struggling to resist the temptation, think of it like a game of hide-and-seek with your phone. Hide it in a drawer, leave it in another room, or even give it to a friend for safekeeping. It's like locking away the *jalebis* when you're trying to avoid temptation – out of sight, out of mind, right?

Speaking of temptation, remember that time Rahul posted a picture of himself at a fancy restaurant, enjoying a five-course meal with Michelin-star chefs? You were instantly hit with a wave of FOMO, even though you had just finished a delicious home-cooked meal.

You started questioning your culinary skills, wondering if your dal-chawal could ever compete with Rahul's gourmet extravaganza. You even contemplated ordering takeout, just to feel like you were part of the cool crowd.

But then you remembered, yaar, that food isn't just about fancy plating and exotic ingredients. It's about nourishment, comfort, and the love that goes into cooking it. Your simple dal-chawal, made with love by your mom, was just as satisfying, if not more so, than Rahul's Michelin-star meal.

So, the next time you see someone on social media enjoying a lavish lifestyle, remember that it's just one aspect of their life. It doesn't define their happiness or their self-worth. And it certainly doesn't mean that your own life is any less fulfilling or meaningful.

Remember, yaar, social media is like a box of mithai – a little bit is enjoyable, but too much can give you a tummy ache. So, enjoy it in moderation, savor the sweet moments, and don't let it spoil your appetite for the real feast that life has to offer.

And speaking of mithai, remember that time Rahul posted a picture of himself devouring a box of kaju katli at a family wedding? You couldn't help but chuckle, knowing full well that he was probably regretting that sugar rush a few hours later.

But then again, who can resist the allure of kaju katli, especially at a big fat Indian wedding? It's like a Bollywood dance sequence for your taste buds, a whirlwind of sweetness, crunch, and pure indulgence.

But just like those dance sequences that leave you breathless and sweaty, indulging in too much social media can also leave you feeling drained and empty. It's like a sugar rush followed by a sugar crash, leaving you with nothing but a lingering sense of dissatisfaction.

So, the next time you find yourself mindlessly scrolling through your feed, craving that next hit of dopamine, remind yourself of Rahul and his kaju katli adventure. Remember that the fleeting pleasure of social media validation is nothing compared to the lasting satisfaction of living a real, authentic life.

It's about finding joy in the simple things, like spending time with loved ones, pursuing your hobbies, or simply enjoying a cup of chai and a good conversation. It's about disconnecting from the virtual world and reconnecting with the real world, the one where you can feel the warmth of the sun on your face, the wind in your hair, and the laughter of your friends ringing in your ears.

Because at the end of the day, yaar, life isn't about how many likes you get or how many followers you have. It's about the memories you create, the relationships you nurture, and the impact you make on the world. It's about living a life that's rich in experiences, not just in virtual likes.

Remember, even Gabbar Singh, the menacing villain of "Sholay," had his moments of vulnerability, muttering "Kitne aadmi the?" in a rare display of fear. Similarly, the seemingly perfect lives portrayed on social media often hide insecurities, anxieties, and struggles that we may never see.

So, the next time you feel the urge to compare yourself to others on social media, take a step back and remind yourself that you're only seeing a tiny fraction of their lives. You're not seeing the sleepless nights, the failed attempts, the tears shed behind closed doors.

Think of it like a Bollywood movie, where the villain always seems invincible until the hero discovers their weakness. Similarly, the seemingly perfect lives on social media often have cracks in their facade, vulnerabilities that are hidden from the public eye.

So, instead of comparing your behind-the-scenes footage to someone else's highlight reel, focus on your own journey, your own growth, your own unique story. Remember, you're the hero of your own life, not a supporting actor in someone else's social media saga.

And just like every Bollywood movie needs a good ending, your social media journey can also have a happy ending. It's about finding a balance, setting healthy boundaries, and using social media as a tool for connection and inspiration, rather than a source of comparison and insecurity.

So, let's rewrite the script, yaar. Let's turn this Squid Game of Social Media into a celebration of our own unique stories, a platform for lifting each other up, a virtual space where we can connect, share, and inspire.

Let's create a social media world that's less about likes and followers, and more about genuine connection, meaningful conversations, and real-life experiences. Because, at the end of the day, the true currency of life isn't virtual likes, it's the love, laughter, and memories we create with the people we care about.

So, what can we, the aam aadmi of the digital age, do to break free from the clutches of this virtual Squid Game? Well, my friend, here are a few tried and tested strategies, straight from the playbook of life:

- **Set Boundaries, Like a Strict School Teacher:**

Remember those teachers who wouldn't let you even whisper during class? It's time to channel your inner disciplinarian and set some strict boundaries for your social media use. Decide on a fixed amount of time each day that you'll allow yourself to scroll through your feed, and then stick to it like Fevicol.

- **Unplug and Recharge, Like a Weekend Getaway:**

Just like we need a break from the daily grind to recharge our batteries, our minds too need a break from the constant barrage of information and stimulation that social media provides. So, schedule regular digital detoxes, where you switch off your phone, put away your laptop, and engage in activities that nourish your soul. It could be anything from reading a book, going for a walk in nature, or simply spending time with loved ones.

- **Curate Your Feed, Like a Masterchef:**

Don't let your social media feed become a buffet of negativity and comparison. Instead, curate it like a masterchef curates their menu, choosing only the most delicious and nourishing ingredients. Unfollow accounts that trigger negative emotions, and follow those that inspire, motivate, and make you laugh. Fill your feed with positive vibes, uplifting stories, and content that adds value to your life.

- **Find Real Connections, Like a Bollywood Rom-Com:**

Remember, social media is just a tool, not a substitute for real human connection. So, put down your phone, step away from the screen, and go out there and meet people in the real world. Have a chai with your friends, go for a walk with your family, or strike up a conversation with a stranger at a coffee shop. You might just discover that the most meaningful connections are made offline, not online.

- **Share Your Real Self, Like a DDLJ Confession:**

Remember that iconic scene in DDLJ where Raj finally confesses his love for Simran on a crowded train platform? Well, social media doesn't have to be all about picture-perfect moments and curated captions. It can also be a platform for sharing your authentic self, your struggles, your triumphs, and everything in between. So, don't be afraid to show your vulnerable side, yaar. Share your stories, your experiences, and your emotions. You might just find that it connects you with others on a deeper level and helps you build more meaningful relationships.

- **Focus on Quality, Not Quantity, Like a Bachchan Dialogue:**

In the world of social media, it's easy to get caught up in the numbers game - the number of likes, comments, shares, and followers. But remember, yaar, it's not about how many people are watching, it's about the impact you're making. So, instead of chasing after vanity metrics, focus on creating quality content that resonates with your audience. Share your passions, your insights, your unique perspective on the world. And remember, just like a Bachchan dialogue that stays with you long after the movie ends, a powerful message can have a lasting impact, even if it doesn't go viral overnight.

- **Remember, It's Just a Game, Yaar:**

Just like any game, social media has its rules, its players, and its winners and losers. But at the end of the day, it's just a game. It's not real life. So, don't take it too seriously.

Don't let it define your worth, your happiness, or your success. Remember, the real game is life itself, and it's a game you can win by focusing on what truly matters - your relationships, your passions, your personal growth, and your own well-being.

Even those dazzling Bollywood celebrities, with their picture-perfect lives and millions of followers, experience moments of vulnerability and self-doubt. Behind the glamorous photoshoots and red-carpet appearances, they too grapple with insecurities, anxieties, and the pressure to maintain a flawless image.

Think of it like Deepika Padukone, who opened up about her battle with depression, or Shah Rukh Khan, who has spoken candidly about his fears and failures. These stars, who we often put on a pedestal, remind us that even the most successful and admired individuals have their own struggles. They're not immune to the pressures of fame, the fear of failure, or the constant scrutiny of the public eye.

Just like us, they have bad days, moments of self-doubt, and times when they feel like they're not good enough. They too get caught up in the comparison game, scrolling through social media and feeling envious of others' seemingly perfect lives. But what sets them apart is their ability to acknowledge those feelings, to seek help when needed, and to ultimately rise above their challenges.

So, the next time you find yourself comparing your life to those you see on social media, remember that you're only seeing a carefully curated version of their reality. You're not seeing the struggles, the insecurities, the behind-the-scenes moments that make them human.

Instead of letting social media fuel your self-doubt, use it as a reminder that we're all in this together. We all have our own unique journeys, our own challenges to overcome, and our own stories to tell. And just like those Bollywood celebrities who have inspired us with their resilience and courage, we too can rise above our struggles and create a life that's truly our own.

Remember, social media, like a Bollywood masala movie, is meant to be entertaining, not a yardstick for your self-worth. It's a platform to showcase your creativity, connect with loved ones, and stay informed, not a competition for the most likes or followers. Just as every character in a movie has a unique role to play, you too have a unique voice and story to share on social media.

So, instead of comparing yourself to the "Ranveer Singhs" and "Deepika Padukones" of the digital world, focus on being the best version of yourself. Let your authenticity shine through, share your passions and interests, and use your voice to uplift and inspire others.

Remember, social media can be a powerful tool for good, a platform for promoting kindness, spreading awareness, and connecting with like-minded individuals. But it can also be a toxic trap if you let it consume your thoughts and emotions.

So, take charge of your social media experience, yaar. Don't let it control you. Use it wisely, set boundaries, and remember that the real world, with all its imperfections and complexities, is far more fulfilling than the curated reality of social media.

Just like a Bollywood movie that teaches us valuable life lessons through its characters and storylines, social media can also be a source of inspiration and learning. But remember, the most important lessons are often found offline, in the real world, in the interactions we have with people, the experiences we have, and the challenges we overcome.

So, step away from the screen, embrace the real world, and remember that your worth is not defined by the number of likes or followers you have. Your worth is inherent, it's in your heart, your mind, and your soul. And that's something that no social media platform can ever take away from you.

Think of self-love like a classic Bollywood love story, where the hero and heroine overcome obstacles and misunderstandings to find their happily ever after. Just as they learn to appreciate each other's strengths and weaknesses, you too must learn to love yourself, flaws and all.

Embrace your quirks, your eccentricities, your unique blend of masala. Celebrate the things that make you different, that set you apart from the crowd. Whether it's your love for Rajma Chawal or your ability to recite dialogues from "Sholay" at the drop of a hat, own it with pride.

Remember, yaar, you're not just a background dancer in the grand Bollywood production of life. You're the star of your own show, the hero of your own story. So, step into the spotlight and shine brightly, my friend. Embrace your individuality, celebrate your uniqueness, and let your self-love light up the world.

Just like a Bollywood movie that leaves you with a smile on your face and a song in your heart, self-love can fill your life with joy, purpose, and meaning. It's about finding your own happy ending, creating a life that's authentically yours, and embracing all the twists and turns along the way.

Just like Raj from "Dilwale Dulhania Le Jayenge," who initially struggled to break free from his carefree bachelor lifestyle to embrace the responsibilities of love and marriage, you too might find it challenging to detach from the allure of social media. It's easy to get caught up in the endless scrolling, the constant stream of updates, and the fear of missing out on the latest trends.

But remember, yaar, just as Raj eventually found the courage to follow his heart and fight for his love, you too have the power to break free from the grip of social media and create a life that's truly fulfilling. It might mean setting limits on your screen time, unfollowing accounts that trigger negative emotions, or simply taking a break from the virtual world to reconnect with the real world.

Remember, the Squid Game of Social Media is not a game you have to play. You can choose to opt out, to create your own rules, to define your own success. You can choose to focus on the things that truly matter - your relationships, your passions, your personal growth, and your well-being.

So, take a deep breath, log off for a while, and step away from the screen. Go out there and experience the real world, the one where you can feel the warmth of the sun on your skin, the wind in your hair, and the laughter of your loved ones filling your ears.

Because at the end of the day, yaar, life is not about how many likes you get or how many followers you have. It's about the memories you create, the connections you make, and the love you share. It's about living a life that's rich in experiences, not just in virtual validation.

Remember, even Basanti, the talkative tangewali from "Sholay," knew when to rein it in and let her actions speak louder than words. In the same way, you don't need to constantly broadcast your every move, thought, or meal on social media. Let your real-life adventures, your genuine connections, and your personal growth speak for themselves.

Just like a Bollywood movie that keeps you guessing until the very end, let your life be a mystery, a suspense thriller that unfolds organically. Don't give away all the spoilers on social media. Save some of the excitement, the intrigue, the magic for real-life interactions.

And when the credits roll, when you look back on your life, let it be a story filled with laughter, love, and meaningful connections, not just a series of filtered selfies and carefully curated posts. Let it be a story that you're proud to share, not just online, but in the hearts of the people who truly matter.

So, dear reader, as you navigate the virtual labyrinth of social media, remember that you are the hero of your own story, the author of your own destiny. Don't let the likes, comments, or follower count dictate your self-worth. Instead, embrace your individuality, celebrate your quirks, and use social media as a tool to connect, inspire, and share your unique voice with the world.

Just like a Bollywood movie that teaches us valuable life lessons through its characters and storylines, let your social media presence be a reflection of your values, your passions, and your dreams. Let it be a platform for spreading positivity, promoting kindness, and building meaningful connections.

And most importantly, remember that the real magic happens offline, in the real world, where you can experience the joy of human connection, the thrill of new adventures, and the simple pleasures of everyday life.

So, log off for a while, put down your phone, and step outside. Go for a walk, have a conversation with a loved one, or simply sit in silence and appreciate the beauty of the world around you.

Because the real Squid Game, my friend, is not the one played on social media. It's the game of life, and it's a game you can win by staying true to yourself, embracing your imperfections, and celebrating the unique beauty of your own story.

Picture this, yaar: You're standing in front of a mirror, staring at your reflection. The harsh fluorescent lights reveal every flaw, every wrinkle, every imperfection. You start to pick yourself apart, focusing on the things you don't like about yourself. Your nose is too big, your eyes are too small, your stomach isn't flat enough.

It's like those moments in Bollywood movies where the heroine breaks down in tears, overwhelmed by self-doubt and insecurity. She questions her worth, her beauty, her ability to be loved.

In those moments, it's easy to forget all the amazing things about yourself, all the qualities that make you special and unique. It's easy to let your inner critic take over, to believe the lies it tells you about your self-worth.

But just like those Bollywood heroines who eventually find their inner strength and embrace their imperfections, you too have the power to silence that negative voice and love yourself unconditionally. It starts with recognizing that you are more than just your physical appearance. You are a complex, multifaceted individual with a rich inner world waiting to be explored.

Think of it like peeling back the layers of an onion, revealing the hidden depths and complexities within. You are not just a pretty face or a toned body. You are a collection of experiences, emotions, thoughts, and dreams. You are a survivor, a fighter, a lover, a dreamer. You are a work of art, a masterpiece in progress.

So, the next time you find yourself staring in the mirror, don't focus on your flaws. Instead, focus on your strengths. Celebrate your achievements, no matter how small they may seem. Remember the times you've made someone laugh, helped someone in need, or simply made the world a brighter place with your presence.

Remember that you are worthy of love, happiness, and success. You are not defined by your flaws or your imperfections. You are defined by your spirit, your courage, your resilience, and your unwavering belief in yourself.

So, embrace your imperfections, yaar. Own them. Celebrate them. Because they are a part of who you are, and they make you all the more beautiful.

Just like those iconic Bollywood characters who have taught us the true meaning of self-acceptance and self-worth, remember that you too have the power to break free from the shackles of self-doubt and embrace your true self. Whether it's Munna Bhai's infectious optimism or Geet's unfiltered zest for life, let their examples inspire you to love yourself unconditionally.

So, yaar, ditch the filters, silence the inner critic, and celebrate your imperfectly perfect self. Remember, you are the hero of your own story, the protagonist of your own Bollywood blockbuster. And just like those unforgettable Bollywood movies that leave you feeling inspired and uplifted, let your life be a masterpiece filled with love, laughter, and unapologetic self-expression.

CHAPTER SEVEN

DALGONA DREAMS: CARVING YOUR PATH

Jugaad, Jugaad, and More Jugaad

Picture this, bro: You're standing in front of a giant honeycomb candy, a dalgona, with a needle in your hand. Your heart is racing, your palms are sweaty, and your mind is racing with a million thoughts. You know that if you don't carve out the perfect shape within the time limit, you're toast. Literally.

It's like that scene In "3 Idiots" where Rancho, Farhan, and Raju are sweating bullets during their final exams, knowing their futures hang in the balance. But instead of giving up, they embrace the challenge, using their wit, ingenuity, and a whole lot of jugaad to ace the test.

Welcome to the Dalgona Dreams chapter, my friend, where we'll explore the art of carving your own path in life, just like those skilled contestants in the Squid Game who meticulously chipped away at their honeycomb candy with laser focus and unwavering determination.

But hold on, yaar, before you start sweating bullets, let me assure you that this isn't about facing life-or-death situations or competing in a deadly game. It's about finding your own unique path, your own "jugaad" to navigate the challenges and obstacles that life throws your way.

Think of it like that time your family was planning a road trip to Goa, but your car broke down on the highway. Instead of panicking, your dad, the ultimate jugaadu, managed to fix the car with a hairpin, a chewing gum wrapper, and a few colorful curses.

That's the spirit we need to embrace, my friend – the spirit of jugaad, the art of improvisation, the ability to find creative solutions to seemingly impossible problems. It's about thinking outside the box, using the resources you have at hand, and never giving up on your dreams.

But hey, this ain't just about fixing broken cars or acing exams. It's about applying that same jugaad spirit to every aspect of your life. It's about finding your own unique path, your own way of doing things, even when the odds are stacked against you.

Just like those "jugaad" moments when you have to make a last-minute birthday cake with Parle-G biscuits and melted chocolate, or fix a leaking pipe with a rubber band and a prayer, life often throws you challenges that require creative problem-solving and a never-say-die attitude.

But here's the twist, my friend: unlike the Squid Game, where one wrong move can cost you your life, the Dalgona Dreams of your life offer you second, third, even fourth chances. You might mess up, you might break the candy, but you can always start again.

Remember, failure is not the end, yaar. It's just a pit stop on your journey to success. It's a chance to learn, to grow, to reinvent yourself. Just like that time you failed your driving test but went on to become a Formula One racer, or that time you bombed a job interview but ended up starting your own successful business.

The key is to embrace your failures, learn from your mistakes, and never give up on your dreams. Because just like those Bollywood heroes who always manage to pull off a last-minute miracle, you too have the power to turn things around.

But let's be real, yaar, carving your own path in life ain't always a smooth ride. It's more like a bumpy auto-rickshaw ride through Chandni Chowk, with potholes, detours, and unexpected obstacles at every turn.

You might face naysayers who tell you your dreams are too big, or too unrealistic. You might encounter setbacks that make you want to give up. You might even doubt yourself, wondering if you have what it takes to succeed.

But remember, yaar, even Rajinikanth started out as a bus conductor. He faced his fair share of struggles and rejections, but he never gave up on his dreams. He kept hustling, kept pushing himself, and eventually became the Thalaivar we all know and love.

So, what's your Dalgona dream, yaar? What's that shape you're trying to carve out of your life's honeycomb candy? Maybe it's starting your own business, like that ambitious chaiwallah who dreamed of becoming a successful entrepreneur. Or maybe it's pursuing your passion for music, like that underdog rapper who rose to fame from the slums of Dharavi.

Whatever your dream may be, remember that you have the power to make it a reality. It might not be easy, it might not be straightforward, but with the right mindset and a little bit of jugaad, you can achieve anything you set your mind to.

Think of it like that scene in "Lage Raho Munna Bhai" where Munna and Circuit embark on a mission to spread Gandhigiri, a philosophy of nonviolence and compassion. They faced ridicule and opposition, but they persevered, using their unique brand of humor and heart to change the world, one act of kindness at a time.

Similarly, your journey towards your Dalgona dream might not be easy. You might face setbacks, challenges, and moments of self-doubt. But as long as you stay true to your values, embrace your creativity, and never lose sight of your goal, you will eventually carve out your own path to success.

And remember, yaar, just like those Bollywood movies that teach us valuable life lessons through their stories, your journey towards your Dalgona dream can also be a source of inspiration and learning for others. So, don't be afraid to share your story, your struggles, your triumphs.

Inspire others with your resilience, your creativity, and your unwavering belief in yourself. And who knows, you might just become the next Bollywood hero, the next inspiration for millions of dreamers out there.

So, yaar, what are you waiting for? Grab that needle, take a deep breath, and start carving. Your Dalgona dream is waiting to be realized. Remember, it's not about perfection, it's about progress. It's not about following the crowd, it's about creating your own path. And most importantly, it's not about giving up, it's about finding your own unique jugaad to overcome any obstacle that comes your way.

Think of it like that scene in "Chak De! India" where Kabir Khan, the disgraced coach, leads a ragtag team of women hockey players to victory. He didn't have the best resources, the most talented players, or the most supportive environment. But he had passion, determination, and a belief in his team's potential.

Similarly, you might not have all the resources or advantages in the world, but you have something far more valuable – your own unique talents, your own creative spirit, and your own unwavering determination to succeed.

So, channel your inner Kabir Khan, yaar. Gather your team of supporters, your friends, family, mentors, and anyone else who believes in you. And then, go out there and chase your dreams with everything you've got.

Remember, the world is your oyster, your canvas, your dalgona. It's up to you to carve out the masterpiece that is your life. So, let your creativity flow, your passion ignite, and your spirit soar.

And just like those iconic Bollywood movies that leave us with a message of hope and inspiration, let your story be one that motivates and uplifts others. Let it be a testament to the power of dreams, the resilience of the human spirit, and the limitless possibilities that lie ahead when you dare to carve your own path.

Picture this, yaar: A small-town girl named Kavya dreams of making it big in Bollywood. She's got the moves, the looks, and the ambition, but she lacks the connections and resources to break into the industry. She auditions for countless roles, faces rejection after rejection, and starts to lose hope.

Her friends and family urge her to give up on her "filmy" dreams and settle for a more stable career. But Kavya refuses to let go of her dalgona dream. She knows that she has something special to offer, a unique talent that deserves to be seen and appreciated.

So, she starts attending acting workshops, networking with industry insiders, and creating her own short films to showcase her skills. She faces numerous obstacles along the way – financial constraints, lack of support, and the constant pressure to conform to societal expectations. But she perseveres, fueled by her passion and unwavering belief in herself.

Kavya's journey is a testament to the power of jugaad, the art of making things happen with limited resources and creative solutions. Just like those local artists who transform scrap materials into stunning works of art, Kavya used her ingenuity and resourcefulness to create opportunities for herself.

She didn't wait for Bollywood to come knocking on her door; she went out there and created her own path. She didn't let her lack of connections or resources deter her; she found ways to network, collaborate, and build her own brand.

And her persistence paid off. One of her short films went viral, catching the eye of a renowned Bollywood director. He was impressed by her talent and offered her a role in his upcoming film. Kavya's dream was finally coming true.

But her story doesn't end there, yaar. It's just the beginning. Because Kavya's journey is a reminder that even the most ambitious dreams can be achieved with the right mindset, a little bit of jugaad, and an unwavering belief in yourself.

So, the next time you feel like giving up on your dreams, remember Kavya's story. Remember that you too have the power to carve your own path, to overcome obstacles, and to create a life that's truly extraordinary.

Just like Kavya, you might not have all the resources or advantages in the world, but you have something far more valuable – your own unique talents, your own creative spirit, and your own unwavering determination to succeed.

So, what's stopping you, yaar? What's the one thing that's been holding you back from chasing your dreams, from carving your own unique path in life? Is it the fear of failure, the lack of resources, or simply the overwhelming feeling of not knowing where to start?

Remember, just like Kavya, who faced rejection and self-doubt, you too might encounter obstacles along the way. But don't let those setbacks define you. Don't let them dim your spark or extinguish your flame.

Instead, embrace them as opportunities for growth, for learning, for discovering your own hidden strengths and resilience. Remember, even the biggest Bollywood blockbusters have their share of dramatic twists and turns, unexpected setbacks, and nail-biting cliffhangers.

But it's in those moments of adversity that the true heroes emerge, the ones who refuse to give up, who fight tooth and nail for their dreams, who ultimately emerge victorious against all odds.

So, channel your inner hero, yaar. Unleash your creativity, your passion, your determination. Embrace the challenges, learn from your mistakes, and never lose sight of your goals.

And remember, just like those Bollywood movies that leave us with a sense of hope and inspiration, your journey of carving your own path can also be a source of motivation for others. So, share your story, your struggles, your triumphs. Inspire others with your resilience, your creativity, and your unwavering belief in yourself.

Because, my friend, you are not just a spectator in this game of life. You are the player, the creator, the artist. You have the power to shape your own destiny, to paint your own masterpiece, to write your own Bollywood blockbuster.

So, what are you waiting for? The stage is set, the spotlight is on you, and the world is eagerly awaiting your performance. Go out there and show them what you're made of, yaar!

Just like those mouth-watering chaat stalls in the market, each with its unique blend of spices and flavors, you too have a unique combination of qualities that make you special.

Don't be afraid to experiment, to try new things, to explore different avenues of your personality. You might be surprised to discover hidden talents, passions, or interests that you never knew existed. Just like that time you accidentally stumbled upon a hidden gem of a book shop in a narrow alleyway, or that time you discovered your hidden talent for singing at a karaoke night with friends, life is full of unexpected surprises.

So, don't be afraid to step out of your comfort zone, yaar. Take a chance, try something new, and see where it leads you. You might just discover a hidden passion, a new hobby, or a different side of yourself that you never knew existed.

And remember, just like those street food vendors who take pride in their creations, you too should be proud of who you are, what you've achieved, and the unique flavor you bring to the world.

Don't let anyone tell you that you're not good enough, not smart enough, or not successful enough. You are enough, just as you are.

So, the next time you feel that pang of self-doubt, that nagging feeling of inadequacy, remind yourself of all the amazing things you've accomplished, all the challenges you've overcome, and all the people whose lives you've touched. Remember that you are a work in progress, a constant evolution, a never-ending story.

And just like those colorful murals that adorn the walls of our cities, your life is a vibrant tapestry of experiences, emotions, and memories. Embrace the colors, the textures, the imperfections, and let your story be a masterpiece that inspires and uplifts others.

Kavya's journey isn't unique, yaar. It's a reflection of the countless stories of ordinary individuals who dared to dream big and carve their own path in life. Take, for instance, the story of Dhirubhai Ambani, who started out as a spice trader and went on to build one of India's largest conglomerates. Or the story of Kiran Mazumdar-Shaw, who founded Biocon, India's leading biotechnology company, despite facing numerous challenges and setbacks.

These are not just stories of success, yaar. They are stories of resilience, of determination, of the unwavering belief in one's own abilities. They are stories of jugaad, of finding innovative solutions to overcome obstacles, of turning challenges into opportunities.

So, the next time you feel like your dreams are too big or your goals are too far-fetched, remember the stories of these real-life heroes. Remember that they too started from humble beginnings, faced their share of struggles, and yet, managed to achieve greatness through their hard work, perseverance, and unwavering spirit.

And just like those inspiring stories of courage and determination that we hear on the news or read about in books, your own journey towards your Dalgona dream can also be a source of inspiration for others. It can be a testament to the power of the human spirit, the ability to overcome adversity, and the limitless possibilities that lie ahead when we dare to chase our dreams.

But remember, yaar, carving your own path isn't just about achieving external success. It's also about finding inner fulfillment, about living a life that's true to your values and passions. It's about discovering your own unique purpose and making a positive impact on the world.

So, don't let fear or doubt hold you back. Embrace the challenges, learn from your mistakes, and keep moving forward. Remember, your Dalgona dream is waiting to be realized. And with a little bit of jugaad, a whole lot of determination, and a sprinkle of self-belief, you can carve out a path that's truly yours.

Think of it like that street vendor who sets up shop every day, rain or shine, with a smile on his face and a twinkle in his eye. He doesn't know how many customers he'll get or how much he'll earn, but he shows up every day, ready to share his delicious chaat with the world. That's the kind of unwavering spirit we need to cultivate in our pursuit of our dreams.

Remember, the path to success isn't always a straight line, yaar. It's more like a Mumbai local train journey, full of unexpected stops, sudden changes in direction, and a whole lot of jostling and pushing. But just like those seasoned commuters who navigate the chaos with ease, you too can learn to adapt, adjust, and find your footing in the ever-changing landscape of life.

So, the next time you encounter a roadblock, a setback, or a moment of self-doubt, don't give up. Instead, take a deep breath, tap into your inner jugaadu, and find a creative solution. Remember, even the most challenging situations can be overcome with a little bit of ingenuity, a dash of perseverance, and a whole lot of heart.

And just like those heartwarming Bollywood movies that leave us with a tear in our eye and a smile on our face, your journey towards your Dalgona dream will have its share of emotional moments. There will be times when you feel like giving up, when you question your abilities, when you wonder if it's all worth it.

But in those moments of vulnerability, remember the stories of those who came before you, the countless individuals who faced their fears, chased their dreams, and emerged victorious. Remember the resilience of the human spirit, the power of perseverance, and the unwavering belief that anything is possible when you set your mind to it.

Consider the story of Private James Martin, a young soldier from the trenches of World War I. Amidst the constant barrage of shells and the ever-present threat of death, James found solace in a most unexpected way – by knitting. Yes, you heard that right, knitting!

In the midst of the chaos and carnage, James would pull out his needles and yarn, creating intricate patterns and designs. He wasn't just knitting scarves or socks, he was knitting a piece of his own sanity, a way to escape the horrors of war and find a moment of peace and creativity.

His fellow soldiers initially mocked him, calling him "granny" and questioning his masculinity. But soon, they started to see the value in his hobby. James's knitting not only kept him occupied but also provided a much-needed distraction from the constant fear and anxiety that plagued the trenches.

As word spread of James's unusual hobby, he became a source of inspiration for his fellow soldiers. Some even started to learn how to knit themselves, finding solace and comfort in the rhythmic movement of the needles and the creation of something beautiful.

James's story is a reminder that even in the darkest of times, when the world seems to be falling apart, we can find ways to nurture our creativity, to express ourselves, and to find moments of joy and peace.

Just like James, who found solace in knitting amidst the chaos of war, you too can find your own "jugaad" to deal with the challenges of life. It might be painting, writing, singing, dancing, or simply spending time in nature.

Remember, self-care isn't a luxury, yaar. It's a necessity. It's what allows you to recharge your batteries, to replenish your energy, and to face the world with renewed vigor. So, don't neglect your own well-being in the pursuit of your dreams. Take time for yourself, indulge in activities that bring you joy, and remember that even the smallest moments of happiness can make a big difference.

Just like those old Hindi film songs that tug at our heartstrings and remind us of the simple joys of life, self-love is about finding happiness in the little things. It's about enjoying a cup of cutting chai with your friends at a roadside stall, watching the sun set over the horizon, or dancing to the latest Bollywood hits at a wedding. It's about finding joy in the everyday moments, appreciating the beauty that surrounds us, and cherishing the simple pleasures that life has to offer.

Imagine a young artist named Maya, struggling to make ends meet in the bustling city of Mumbai. She spends her days working odd jobs, her evenings attending art classes, and her nights dreaming of showcasing her work in a gallery. But the road to success is paved with rejection and disappointment.

Maya faces numerous rejections from galleries, art critics dismiss her work as "amateurish," and she starts to doubt her own talent. The weight of her struggles feels heavy on her shoulders, like a leaden backpack filled with unsold paintings.

But Maya, with her unwavering spirit and artistic soul, refuses to give up. She finds solace in her art, using her paintbrush as a weapon against her self-doubt. She paints her emotions, her frustrations, her dreams onto the canvas, turning her pain into something beautiful.

One day, while showcasing her art at a local market, a renowned art collector notices her work. He's captivated by her raw talent, her unique style, and the emotions that emanate from her paintings. He offers her a solo exhibition at his gallery, and Maya's career takes off.

But the real victory for Maya isn't the fame or recognition. It's the newfound confidence in her own abilities, the unwavering belief in her artistic vision, and the deep sense of fulfillment she derives from her work.

Because just as "Dil Chahta Hai" taught us about the importance of friendship and following your heart, so too can your own tribe of friends and family be the wind beneath your wings. They'll be there to catch you when you fall, cheer you on when you succeed, and remind you of your worth when you forget. Surround yourself with those who uplift you, inspire you, and believe in your Dalgona dream.

But what if your dream feels more like a tangled ball of wool than a perfectly shaped dalgona? What if it's constantly changing, evolving, or even disappearing altogether? Well, yaar, that's okay too. Just like those impromptu dance sequences in Bollywood movies, where the choreography changes on a whim and the dancers improvise on the spot, your dream can also take unexpected turns and detours.

The important thing is to stay flexible, to adapt to the changing circumstances, and to keep moving forward, even when the path ahead seems unclear. Remember, even the most seasoned travelers get lost sometimes. But with a little bit of resourcefulness, a dash of courage, and a whole lot of "jugaad," you can always find your way back on track.

So, embrace the uncertainty, yaar. Let your dream evolve, morph, and transform. Don't be afraid to experiment, to try new things, to explore different avenues.

And who knows, you might just discover a hidden passion, a hidden talent, or a new direction that takes your life to a whole new level.

Think of your life as a Bollywood movie set, where you are both the director and the star. You get to choose the script, the cast, and the soundtrack. You have the power to create a blockbuster hit filled with laughter, love, and unforgettable adventures.

So, don't let fear or self-doubt hold you back, yaar. Embrace the chaos, unleash your creativity, and let your "jugaad" spirit shine. Carve your own path, follow your own rhythm, and create a life that's as unique and vibrant as you are.

Remember, your Dalgona dream is not just a fantasy, it's a possibility waiting to be realized. So, grab your tools, muster your courage, and start carving. The world is your canvas, your life is your masterpiece, and the only limit is your imagination.

And just like those iconic Bollywood dialogues that leave a lasting impression, let me leave you with this thought: "Apna time aayega, yaar!" (Your time will come!). So, keep hustling, keep dreaming, and keep believing in yourself.

Because when you combine your passion with perseverance and a dash of "jugaad," you become an unstoppable force, a true Bollywood hero in the making.

CHAPTER EIGHT

VIPs & BFFs: Choosing Your Circle

Apna Time Aayega, But With the Right Crew

Imagine this, : You're at a swanky Bollywood party, surrounded by glitz, glamour, and a sea of familiar faces. The air is thick with the scent of expensive perfume and the clinking of champagne glasses. You spot Karan Johar in one corner, deep in conversation with a superstar, while Manish Malhotra is busy air-kissing socialites.

But amidst all the glitz and glamour, you feel a sense of unease. You don't quite fit in with the crowd, you don't understand the inside jokes, and you feel like you're on the outside looking in. It's like being the only one who hasn't seen the latest Dharma Productions blockbuster – everyone else is talking about it, but you're left feeling lost and out of the loop.

Welcome to the VIP section of life, my friend, where the stakes are high, the competition is fierce, and the pressure to belong is intense. It's a world where everyone seems to be vying for the attention of the "VIPs" – the rich, the famous, the powerful – hoping to bask in their reflected glory and gain a foothold In the exclusive inner circle.

But hey, don't worry, yaar. We've all been there. We've all felt that pang of envy when we see our friends rubbing shoulders with the who's who of society, attending exclusive events, and living the high life.

It's like that time your college buddy landed a job at a top multinational company and started posting pictures of his swanky office, business trips abroad, and fancy dinners with clients. You couldn't help but feel a twinge of jealousy, wondering why you weren't as successful, as connected, as "important" as him.

But here's the thing, my friend: the VIP section of life isn't all it's cracked up to be. It's a world of superficiality, where appearances matter more than substance, where connections are often transactional, and where loyalty is a rare commodity.

Think of it like those Bollywood award shows where everyone is smiling for the cameras, but behind the scenes, there's backstabbing, gossip, and a constant struggle for power and recognition. It's a world where friendships are often based on convenience, where alliances are formed and broken with alarming frequency, and where trust is a fragile thing.

So, the question is, yaar, do you want to be a VIP or a BFF? Do you want to chase after the elusive approval of the elite, or do you want to cultivate genuine connections with people who truly care about you? Do you want to be a part of the in-crowd, or do you want to build your own tribe of like-minded individuals who share your values and support your dreams?

It's like choosing between a plate of fancy sushi at a Michelin-star restaurant and a home-cooked meal with your family. Sure, the sushi might look more aesthetically pleasing and impress your Instagram followers, but the warmth and love you feel sharing a meal with your loved ones is priceless.

Similarly, the connections you forge with your true friends, your BFFs, are far more valuable than any fleeting association with the VIPs of the world. Your BFFs are the ones who know you inside out, who accept you for who you are, who will be there for you through thick and thin, no matter what.

They are your Raj and Simran, your Jai and Veeru, your Rancho, Farhan, and Raju. They are the ones who make you laugh until your sides hurt, who offer a shoulder to cry on when you're feeling down, and who cheer you on as you chase your dreams.

So, the next time you find yourself feeling envious of someone else's social circle, remember that true friendship isn't about status, fame, or fortune. It's about genuine connection, mutual respect, and unwavering support.

It's about finding your tribe, your people, those who get you, who appreciate your quirks, and who love you for who you are. It's about building a circle of trust, loyalty, and unwavering friendship that will last a lifetime.

Remember, your tribe isn't just about the number of people who follow you on Instagram or like your Facebook posts. It's about the quality of those connections, the depth of those relationships, and the mutual support and encouragement that you share. It's about finding your own "Dil Chahta Hai" gang, those few special individuals who get you, who accept you for who you are, and who will always be there for you, no matter what.

Think of it like building your own cricket team, where each player brings their own unique skills and strengths to the table. You need a captain who can lead, a batsman who can score runs, a bowler who can take wickets, and a fielder who can catch those impossible catches. Similarly, your tribe should be a diverse group of individuals who complement each other's strengths and weaknesses, who challenge you to grow, and who support you in your pursuit of your dreams.

But just like a cricket team needs a good coach to guide and motivate them, you too need mentors and role models who can inspire you and help you navigate the ups and downs of life. Look up to those who have achieved what you aspire to, who have carved their own path, who have overcome obstacles and emerged victorious.

Learn from their experiences, their mistakes, and their successes. Seek their guidance, their wisdom, and their support. Remember, even the greatest players need a coach to help them reach their full potential.

So, yaar, don't be afraid to reach out to those who inspire you. Ask for advice, seek mentorship, and learn from those who have already walked the path you're on. They can offer valuable insights, support, and encouragement that can help you navigate the challenges and achieve your goals.

And remember, just like those Bollywood movies that teach us the importance of family, your loved ones are your biggest cheerleaders, your most loyal supporters, and your unwavering source of strength. They might not always understand your dreams or your choices, but they'll always be there for you, through thick and thin.

So, cherish those relationships, yaar. Nurture them, invest in them, and never take them for granted. Because at the end of the day, it's the love and support of your family and friends that will truly make your life a blockbuster hit.

And just as every blockbuster needs a catchy soundtrack, your life needs a playlist that celebrates YOU. So ditch the chart-toppers that everyone else is listening to and create your own playlist filled with songs that resonate with your soul. It might be a mix of old Bollywood classics, peppy Punjabi numbers, or even a few soulful ghazals. Let the music be a reflection of your unique personality, your quirks, your dreams, and your aspirations.

Remember, yaar, life is too short to live someone else's dream or follow someone else's script. It's your story, your journey, your masterpiece. So, grab the pen, take charge of the narrative, and write a story that's filled with passion, purpose, and a whole lot of Bollywood-style drama.

And when the curtains fall, when the credits roll, and you look back on your life, let it be a story that you're proud of, a story that makes you smile, a story that inspires others. Let it be a story that says, "I lived my life on my own terms, I chased my dreams, I embraced my flaws, and I found happiness in the most unexpected places."

Because at the end of the day, yaar, that's what truly matters. It's not the number of likes you get or the size of your social circle. It's about living a life that's true to yourself, a life that's filled with love, laughter, and meaningful connections.

So, go on, my friend. Take that first step, embrace the unknown, and write your own blockbuster story.

Now, let's talk about our buddy Rahul, the self-proclaimed "Instagram King." This dude is a social media ninja, posting stories, reels, and selfies faster than you can say "filter." He's always at the hottest parties, rubbing shoulders with the who's who of the city, and his feed is a never-ending stream of envy-inducing experiences.

But one day, Rahul confided in you, his voice laced with a hint of sadness. "Yaar," he said, "I feel like I'm living in a bubble. I'm surrounded by all these people, but I feel so alone. It's like everyone is just putting on a show, trying to impress each other. There's no real connection, no genuine friendship."

Rahul, the master of the virtual world, was feeling lost in the real world. He had thousands of followers, but he couldn't name a single person he could truly call a friend. He had a feed full of likes and comments, but he was starving for genuine human connection.

His story is a reminder that social media, while a powerful tool for connecting with others, can also create a false sense of intimacy and belonging. It's easy to get caught up in the numbers game, the constant pursuit of validation and approval, and forget that true friendship is built on trust, vulnerability, and shared experiences.

So, what did Rahul do? He decided to take a break from the virtual world and reconnect with the real world. He started spending more time with his family, rekindling old friendships, and pursuing his hobbies. He started volunteering at a local NGO, using his social media skills to promote their cause.

And guess what, yaar? He found his tribe, his people, those who genuinely cared about him, not just his online persona. He discovered that true happiness comes not from the number of likes or followers you have, but from the quality of your relationships, the depth of your connections, and the joy you find in giving back to others.

Rahul's story is a reminder that the true VIPs in our lives are not the ones with the most followers or the fanciest parties, but the ones who stick with us through thick and thin, the ones who know our flaws and love us anyway, the ones who make us laugh until our sides hurt and offer a shoulder to cry on when we need it most.

It's like that scene in "Rang De Basanti" where a group of friends bond over their shared experiences, their love for their country, and their unwavering loyalty to each other. They might not be the most popular or the most successful, but they have something far more valuable – a genuine connection that transcends social status, wealth, and popularity.

So, the next time you find yourself scrolling through your social media feed, feeling envious of those who seem to have it all, remember Rahul's story. Remember that true friendship isn't about likes or comments, it's about shared experiences, mutual support, and unwavering loyalty.

It's about finding your tribe, your people, those who get you, who appreciate your quirks, and who love you for who you are. It's about building a circle of trust, respect, and genuine affection that will last a lifetime.

And just like those unforgettable Bollywood movies that celebrate the power of friendship, let your life be a testament to the importance of surrounding yourself with people who lift you up, inspire you, and make you a better version of yourself.

Remember, yaar, you're not just a player in this game of life. You're the hero, the protagonist, the one who gets to choose your supporting cast. So, choose wisely, my friend. Choose those who will be your BFFs, your partners in crime, your confidantes, and your cheerleaders.

Because at the end of the day, when the lights fade and the music stops, it's the love and support of your true friends that will truly matter. It's the memories you create together, the laughter you share, and the bonds you forge that will last a lifetime.

So, raise a toast to your tribe, yaar. Celebrate those who lift you up, who make you laugh, who inspire you to be a better version of yourself. And just like those epic Bollywood dance numbers that bring everyone together in a joyous celebration, let your friendships be a source of joy, laughter, and unforgettable memories.

Remember, the VIP section of life might seem alluring, but it's the BFF section that truly matters. It's where you'll find the real treasures, the genuine connections, and the love that lasts a lifetime.

So, choose your circle wisely, yaar. Surround yourself with people who make you feel like a superstar, who believe in your dreams, and who celebrate your successes, big or small. Because with the right crew by your side, you can conquer any challenge, overcome any obstacle, and create a life that's truly legendary.

Now, take our buddy Rahul, the social media sensation, for example. He was so busy chasing likes and followers that he forgot to water his own friendships. He was so focused on his virtual image that he neglected his real-life connections. But when he finally took a break from the screen, he realized that the true treasures of life were not found in the virtual world, but in the hearts of the people who loved him.

It's like that time Rahul went on a solo trip to the Himalayas, hoping to find inner peace and enlightenment. He posted pictures of himself meditating by a waterfall, trekking through snow-capped mountains, and sipping tea with a wise old monk. But the truth is, he was bored out of his mind. He missed the hustle and bustle of the city, the gossip sessions with his friends, and the late-night biryani runs.

So, he decided to cut his trip short and head back home. And guess what? He ended up having the time of his life. He reconnected with his childhood friends, discovered hidden gems in his own city, and even found love in the most unexpected place – a local chai stall!

Rahul's story is a reminder that sometimes, the greatest adventures are found not in faraway lands or exotic destinations, but in the simple joys of everyday life. It's about finding happiness in the little things, appreciating the people around you, and living a life that's true to yourself.

So, the next time you find yourself glued to your phone, scrolling through endless feeds of perfectly curated lives, remember Rahul's Himalayan adventure. Remember that true happiness and fulfillment are not found in the virtual world, but in the real world, in the connections we make, the experiences we have, and the moments we cherish.

It's about finding the "jugaad" to balance your virtual and real life, just like our very own Jugaadu Guy from "3 Idiots." This guy could make a functioning vacuum cleaner out of scrap metal and a broken table fan!

Similarly, you can find creative ways to use social media for good, without letting it consume your life. Share your passions, connect with like-minded people, and use your platform to spread positivity and inspiration. But don't forget to unplug every now and then, to step away from the screen and experience the real world in all its messy, chaotic glory.

Remember, the Squid Game of Social Media might be tempting, with its promises of likes, followers, and instant gratification. But the real game, yaar, is the one you play in the real world, the one where you build genuine connections, pursue your passions, and create a life that's truly yours.

So, log off for a while, put down your phone, and step away from the screen. Go out there and live your life, yaar.

Because the real magic happens not in the virtual world, but in the real world, where you can taste the pani puri, feel the sand between your toes, and hear the laughter of your loved ones.

And remember, just like those Bollywood movies that always have a happy ending, your story too can have a happy ending. But it's up to you to write it, yaar. So, grab that pen, ditch the filters, and start living your life, not for the 'gram, but for yourself.

So, ditch those fake friends who only want to use you as a prop in their social media show. Surround yourself with the Circuit's of your life, the ones who will stand by you through thick and thin, the ones who will make you laugh even when you're feeling down, the ones who will remind you of your worth when you forget.

Because, yaar, the VIP section might seem glamorous, but the BFF section is where the real party is at. It's where you can be yourself, where you can let your guard down, where you can find love, acceptance, and support that's deeper than any like or comment.

So, here's to the BFFs, the unsung heroes of our lives, the ones who make life worth living. Let's raise a toast to their unwavering loyalty, their unconditional love, and their infectious laughter. And let's promise to be that kind of friend to others, the kind who doesn't just show up for the photo ops, but who shows up for the real moments, the messy moments, the moments that truly matter.

Because just as Rancho from "3 Idiots" taught us, "Chase excellence, and success will follow," but chase it with your own squad, your own "Chatur Ramalingam" cheering you on (in his own hilarious way). So, find your Rancho,

Farhan, and Raju – the ones who will celebrate your quirks, push you to be your best, and always have your back, even when you're facing your own "Virus."

And hey, just like every Bollywood movie has a dramatic climax, your journey of choosing your circle will also have its share of ups and downs. There might be misunderstandings, disagreements, even betrayals. But just as our favorite on-screen characters learn to forgive, to let go, and to move on, so too must we navigate the complexities of human relationships with compassion and understanding.

Remember, friendships, like any good Bollywood romance, require effort, communication, and a whole lot of "dil." So, invest in your relationships, nurture them with love and care, and don't be afraid to let go of those that no longer serve you.

And as you build your tribe, remember that diversity is key. Just like a Bollywood masala movie with its mix of comedy, drama, and action, your circle of friends should be a vibrant mix of personalities, backgrounds, and interests. This will not only enrich your life with different perspectives and experiences, but it will also challenge you to grow and expand your horizons.

So, open your heart, yaar, and let new people into your life. You never know who might become your next BFF, your partner in crime, your confidante, your biggest supporter.

Because just as Rancho, Farhan, and Raju formed an unbreakable bond that transcended their differences and supported each other's dreams, you too can find your own "3 Idiots" gang – a group of friends who will cheer you on, challenge you to grow, and remind you that success isn't just about grades or job titles, but about living a life that's true to yourself.

So, whether you're a struggling artist like Maya, a social media enthusiast like Rahul, or a dreamer with big ambitions, remember that the people you surround yourself with can make all the difference in your journey. Choose your circle wisely, yaar. Find your tribe, your people, your BFFs, and let them be your guiding light, your support system, and your partners in crime as you navigate the ups and downs of life.

Because at the end of the day, yaar, life is a team sport. And with the right team by your side, you can achieve anything you set your mind to. So, go out there and build your own Bollywood-worthy squad, a group of friends who will make you laugh, cry, dance, and celebrate every moment of this crazy, beautiful journey called life.

Remember, your tribe isn't just about cheering you on, but also about keeping you grounded, like that one friend who always reminds you to eat your greens even when all you want is another plate of butter chicken. They are your compass, your reality check, and your voice of reason. Surround yourself with those who will challenge you to grow, who will call you out on your BS, and who will always have your best interests at heart.

So, as you navigate the choppy waters of life, let your tribe be your lighthouse, guiding you towards your true north. Let them be your anchor, keeping you grounded when the storms of self-doubt threaten to sweep you away. And most importantly, let them be your mirror, reflecting back to you the amazing, unique, and utterly lovable individual that you are.

Because at the end of the day, yaar, life is too short to spend it with people who don't get you, who don't appreciate your quirks, and who don't celebrate your successes. So, choose your circle wisely, my friend. Build a tribe that empowers you, that supports you, and that makes you feel like you can conquer the world, one crazy adventure at a time.

So, while the "VIPs" of the world might have their exclusive clubs and fancy parties, remember that true friendship isn't about social status or material possessions. It's about finding your tribe, your people, those who genuinely care about you and support your dreams.

It's about having a group of friends who will be there for you through thick and thin, who will laugh with you, cry with you, and celebrate your victories, both big and small. It's about building a community of like-minded individuals who share your values, your passions, and your zest for life.

Think of it like building your own personal cricket team, where each member brings their own unique skills and strengths to the table. You need a captain who can lead, a batsman who can score runs, a bowler who can take wickets, and a fielder who can catch those impossible catches. Similarly, your tribe should be a diverse group of individuals who complement each other's strengths and weaknesses, who challenge you to grow, and who support you in your pursuit of your dreams.

But just like a cricket team needs a good coach to guide and motivate them, you too need mentors and role models who can inspire you and help you navigate the ups and downs of life. Look up to those who have achieved what you aspire to, who have carved their own path, who have overcome obstacles and emerged victorious.

Learn from their experiences, their mistakes, and their successes. Seek their guidance, their wisdom, and their support. Remember, even the greatest players need a coach to help them reach their full potential.

So, yaar, don't be afraid to reach out to those who inspire you. Ask for advice, seek mentorship, and learn from those who have already walked the path you're on. They can offer valuable insights, support, and encouragement that can help you navigate the challenges and achieve your goals.

And just as every great Bollywood movie has a memorable ending, so too must we craft our own fulfilling conclusions. The ending of your story isn't just about achieving your goals or reaching a certain level of success. It's about the relationships you've nurtured, the lessons you've learned, and the impact you've made on the world.

It's about looking back on your journey with a sense of pride, knowing that you've stayed true to yourself, that you've surrounded yourself with people who lift you up, and that you've made a positive difference in the lives of others.

So, as you navigate the VIPs and BFFs of life, remember that your "Apna Time Aayega," your time to shine, will come. But it won't come by chasing after the wrong crowd or trying to fit into a mold that doesn't suit you. It will come when you embrace your individuality, surround yourself with those who truly love and support you, and carve your own unique path in this world.

Remember, the real VIPs in your life are the ones who see your worth, who appreciate your quirks, and who love you for who you are, flaws and all. They are the ones who will be there for you through thick and thin, who will celebrate your successes and comfort you in your failures.

So, choose your circle wisely, yaar. Surround yourself with the people who make you laugh, who inspire you to be a better version of yourself, and who make you feel like you can conquer the world. Because with the right crew by your side, your "Apna Time Aayega" will not just be a dream, but a reality.

In the grand tapestry of life, remember that the threads of friendship, love, and support are the ones that truly weave a beautiful and meaningful story. So, cherish those connections, nurture those relationships, and create a legacy that's not just about individual success, but about the collective joy, laughter, and love that you shared with your tribe.

CHAPTER NINE

Your Ending, Your Choice

Happily Ever After? Only If You Write It Yourself !

Picture this: The credits are rolling, the lights come up, and you leave the movie theater feeling a mix of emotions. Was it a happy ending, a tragic one, or something in between? Did the hero get the girl, did the villain get their comeuppance, or was it a cliffhanger leaving you wanting more?

But here's the twist, my friend: This ain't just any Bollywood blockbuster we're talking about. This is the movie of YOUR life, and the ending hasn't been written yet. It's a blank canvas, a wide-open road, a choose-your-own-adventure story waiting for your unique touch.

Think of it like that time you were playing chor-police with your friends in your neighborhood gully. You got to decide whether to be the cunning thief who outsmarted everyone or the brave cop who saved the day. It was your game, your rules, your ending.

Similarly, the ending of your life story is entirely up to you. You get to decide whether it's a tear-jerking melodrama, a laugh-out-loud comedy, or an inspirational tale of triumph over adversity. You get to choose the characters, the plot twists, and the climax.

But just like a Bollywood movie, your ending won't write itself. It requires effort, dedication, and a whole lot of creativity. You need to be the director, the screenwriter, and the lead actor of your own life, making conscious choices, taking bold actions, and embracing the unexpected turns that come your way.

Remember, yaar, the ending of your story isn't just about achieving success or accumulating wealth. It's about living a life that's meaningful, fulfilling, and true to your values. It's about making a positive impact on the world, leaving a legacy that you can be proud of, and ultimately, finding happiness and contentment in your own unique way.

So, yaar, what kind of ending do you envision for yourself? Do you see yourself as a Shah Rukh Khan, finding love and happiness after overcoming countless obstacles? Or maybe you're more like Aamir Khan in "Dangal," achieving success through sheer grit and determination, inspiring generations to come. Perhaps you identify with Sridevi in "English Vinglish," who rediscovers her self-worth and empowers herself through education and self-improvement.

The possibil'ties are endless, just like the variety of roles our beloved Bollywood actors have played over the years. But remember, you're not just playing a role, you're living your life. And just like those iconic characters who have touched our hearts and inspired us, you too have the power to create a story that's both meaningful and memorable.

It all starts with a vision, yaar, a clear picture of what you want your ending to look like. Do you see yourself surrounded by loved ones, enjoying the fruits of your labor? Do you envision yourself making a difference in the world, leaving a lasting legacy that will inspire generations to come? Or maybe you simply want to live a life filled with joy, laughter, and adventure.

Whatever your vision may be, write it down, yaar. Create a storyboard, a blueprint for your life, and then start taking steps to make it a reality. It won't be easy, and there will be plenty of challenges along the way. But remember, even the most epic Bollywood movies have their fair share of villains, plot twists, and heart-wrenching moments.

The key is to persevere, to keep moving forward, to never give up on your dreams. Just like those Bollywood heroes who face seemingly insurmountable odds but ultimately emerge victorious, you too have the strength and resilience to overcome any obstacle that comes your way.

And just like those iconic dialogues that stay with us long after the movie ends, let your life be a testament to the power of hope, the importance of perseverance, and the unwavering belief that you can create your own happily ever after.

So, what kind of ending do you envision for yourself? Do you see yourself surrounded by loved ones, enjoying the fruits of your labor? Do you envision yourself making a difference in the world, leaving a lasting legacy that will inspire generations to come? Or maybe you simply want to live a life filled with joy, laughter, and adventure.

Whatever your vision may be, write it down, yaar. Create a storyboard, a blueprint for your life, and then start taking steps to make it a reality. It won't be easy, and there will be plenty of challenges along the way. But remember, even the most successful individuals have faced setbacks and failures.

The key is to persevere, to keep moving forward, to never give up on your dreams. Just like those who have achieved greatness before you, you too have the strength and resilience to overcome any obstacle that comes your way.

And just as a great novel or an inspiring biography leaves a lasting impression, let your life be a testament to the power of hope, the importance of perseverance, and the unwavering belief that you can create your own happily ever after.

Remember, the ending of your story isn't just about achieving success or accumulating wealth. It's about living a life that's meaningful, fulfilling, and true to your values. It's about making a positive impact on the world, leaving a legacy that you can be proud of, and ultimately, finding happiness and contentment in your own unique way.

Consider the story of Sudha Murty, a woman who dared to defy societal norms and expectations. In a time when women were often confined to the domestic sphere, Sudha pursued her passion for computer science and engineering, eventually becoming the chairperson of Infosys Foundation.

She didn't let societal expectations dictate her path. Instead, she carved her own niche, breaking barriers and inspiring countless women along the way. Her story is a testament to the power of following your own heart, pursuing your passions, and creating a life that's truly your own.

Just like Sudha Murty, you too have the power to break free from societal constraints and create your own unique path. Don't let anyone tell you what you can or cannot do. Follow your heart, chase your dreams, and create a life that makes you proud.

Remember, yaar, your ending is not predetermined. It's a blank canvas, a waiting for you to fill it with your own unique colors and strokes. So, pick up your brush, your pen, your guitar, or whatever tool you choose to express yourself, and start creating your masterpiece.

Think of it like a sports match, where half-time offers a chance to regroup and strategize before the final whistle. Your life too needs those pauses, those moments of reflection where you assess your progress, re-evaluate your goals, and make necessary adjustments. Maybe you need to switch gears, change your strategy, or simply take a break and recharge.

It's okay to hit the pause button. It's okay to take a detour, to explore new avenues, to try different approaches. Don't be afraid to change your mind, to change your course, or even to change your entire game plan.

Remember, the ending is not set in stone. It's a work in progress, a constantly evolving narrative that you have the power to shape and mold.

Embrace the uncertainty. Embrace the challenges, the setbacks, the unexpected twists and turns. Because it's in those moments that you'll discover your true strength, your resilience, and your ability to create your own happily ever after.

And just like those inspiring figures who have overcome adversity and achieved greatness, let me leave you with this thought: "The game isn't over yet, my friend!". So, keep writing, keep dreaming, and keep believing in yourself.

Because your story deserves a standing ovation.

Consider the remarkable life of J.K. Rowling, the author of the beloved Harry Potter series. Before achieving global fame and success, Rowling faced a series of personal and professional setbacks. She was a single mother, struggling financially, battling depression, and dealing with the rejection of her manuscript by numerous publishers.

But Rowling didn't let these challenges define her. She persevered, fueled by her passion for writing and her unwavering belief in her story. She didn't give up on her dream, even when it seemed like the whole world was against her.

She kept writing, kept submitting her manuscript, and eventually, a small publishing house in London took a chance on her. The rest, as they say, is history.

Rowling's story is a powerful reminder that setbacks and failures are not the end of the road, but merely detours on the journey towards our dreams. It's a testament to the power of perseverance, the importance of staying true to your passion, and the unwavering belief in yourself, even when the odds are stacked against you.

So, the next time you feel like giving up on your dreams, remember J.K. Rowling's story. Remember that every rejection, every setback, every obstacle is simply a test of your resilience, a challenge to overcome.

Embrace the detours, yaar. Learn from your mistakes, and never lose sight of your goal. Because just like Rowling, who transformed her life through the power of her imagination and perseverance, you too have the ability to create your own magic, your own happily ever after.

Imagine this, yaar: A young woman named Joanne Rowling is sitting in a cozy cafe, scribbling away in a notebook. She's a single mother, struggling to make ends meet, working odd jobs to support herself and her daughter. But in those stolen moments, amidst the chaos of daily life, she's creating a magical world filled with witches, wizards, and fantastical creatures.

She's writing the first Harry Potter book, unaware that it will one day become a global phenomenon, beloved by millions of readers around the world. But the road to success isn't easy. She faces rejection after rejection, with publishers telling her that children's books don't sell, that fantasy isn't marketable, that her dreams are simply too big.

But Joanne, like a true Gryffindor, refuses to give up. She perseveres, driven by her passion for storytelling and her unwavering belief in her own creation. She spends countless hours in libraries, cafes, and even on park benches, writing and rewriting her manuscript until it's finally accepted by a small publishing house.

And the rest, as they say, is history. Harry Potter becomes a global phenomenon, spawning a series of books, movies, theme parks, and a whole universe of magic and wonder.

Joanne Rowling's story is a testament to the power of perseverance, the importance of staying true to your dreams, and the magic that happens when you refuse to give up on yourself. It's a reminder that even in the face of adversity, even when the odds seem stacked against you, you can achieve anything you set your mind to.

So, the next time you feel like your dreams are too big or your goals are too far-fetched, remember Joanne Rowling's story. Remember that she too started out as a struggling single mother, with nothing but a dream and a typewriter.

Remember that she faced rejection and hardship, but she never gave up. She kept writing, kept believing, and eventually, her dream came true.

Her story doesn't end with a simple book deal, yaar. Imagine Joanne, manuscript in hand, now facing a new set of challenges. Publishers wanted to market her book with a male pseudonym, believing a female author wouldn't appeal to young boys. But Joanne, with her Gryffindor courage, refused to compromise her identity. She insisted on using her own name, even adding a middle initial 'K' (for Kathleen) to make it sound more ambiguous.

Even after the first Harry Potter book was published, the struggle continued. It wasn't an instant bestseller. It took time, word-of-mouth recommendations, and a sprinkle of luck for the wizarding world to truly capture hearts around the globe. Through it all, Joanne remained resilient, her belief in her creation unwavering.

Her story is a masterclass in embracing the "jugaad" spirit. With limited resources and countless rejections, she found ways to get her story out there, proving that sometimes, the most unconventional paths lead to the most extraordinary destinations. Just like those old wives' tales that somehow always seem to work, or that one weird trick your grandmother used to fix everything from a broken heart to a leaky tap, Rowling's journey reminds us that sometimes, the most unlikely solutions can lead to the most magical outcomes.

So, yaar, take a page out of Joanne's book (pun intended!). Don't be afraid to embrace your unique voice, your quirky ideas, your unconventional dreams. Don't let setbacks deter you, rejections define you, or naysayers discourage you.

Remember, your Dalgona dream isn't just about achieving external success, it's about staying true to yourself, your passions, and your beliefs. It's about finding your own magic, your own way of making a difference in the world.

Just like MK Gandhi, who used his simple dhoti and unwavering principles to challenge an empire, you too can harness your own unique strengths and values to create a life that's truly extraordinary. It might not be as grand as leading a nation to independence, but it could be as simple as standing up for what you believe in, pursuing your passions, or making a positive impact on your community.

Remember, your ending is not predetermined by your circumstances, your background, or the expectations of others. It's a blank slate, waiting for you to write your own story. It's a canvas, yearning for your vibrant colors and bold strokes.

So, pick up your metaphorical pen, yaar, and start writing. Craft a story that's filled with purpose, passion, and a whole lot of "jugaad." A story that celebrates your individuality, your quirks, your triumphs, and your failures. A story that inspires others, that leaves a lasting legacy, and that ultimately leads you to a fulfilling and joyful ending.

Think of it like a classic Bollywood masala movie, filled with drama, romance, action, and a healthy dose of comedy. Your life story can be just as entertaining, just as inspiring, and just as impactful. But it's up to you to write the script, yaar. It's up to you to cast the characters, to create the plot twists, and to direct the grand finale.

So, take a deep breath, tap into your creativity, and let your imagination run wild. Because your ending, your choice, your happily ever after is waiting to be written. And just like those unforgettable Bollywood movies that leave us with a smile on our faces and a song in our hearts, let your life be a masterpiece that's worth watching again and again.

But hey, just like a Bollywood movie wouldn't be complete without a few naach-gaana sequences, your life's ending needs a soundtrack too! So, crank up the volume and let the music move you. Whether it's the soulful tunes of Kishore Kumar or the peppy beats of Badshah, let the melodies fill your heart with joy and inspire you to dance to your own rhythm.

Remember, your ending doesn't have to be a grand finale with fireworks and confetti. It can be as simple as finding contentment in a quiet corner of a library, surrounded by your favorite books, or as adventurous as trekking through the Himalayas, your heart filled with the thrill of the unknown.

It's about creating an ending that resonates with your soul, that reflects your values, your passions, and your dreams. It's about living a life that's authentically yours, a life that you can look back on with pride and satisfaction. Remember, your ending isn't just about crossing the finish line or achieving a certain goal. It's about the journey, the lessons learned, the relationships formed, and the impact you've made along the way. It's about looking back at your life and feeling a sense of satisfaction, knowing that you lived it on your own terms, that you chased your dreams, that you loved fiercely, and that you left a mark on the world.

Think of it like a grand Diwali celebration, where the lights twinkle, the music fills the air, and the aroma of delicious food fills your senses. Your life's ending should be a celebration of all that you've accomplished, all that you've experienced, and all that you've become.

It should be a time to reflect on the challenges you've overcome, the friendships you've cherished, and the love you've shared. It should be a time to look back with gratitude, knowing that you've lived a life that's full of meaning and purpose.

So, as you write the final chapter of your story, remember to include all the elements that make it uniquely yours. Sprinkle in a dash of humor, a pinch of adventure, and a generous dose of love. Let your story be a reflection of your values, your passions, and your dreams.

And most importantly, yaar, don't forget to add a touch of magic. Just like those unexpected plot twists that make Bollywood movies so captivating, your life too is full of surprises, serendipitous moments, and unexpected turns.

Embrace the uncertainty, welcome the unexpected, and let the magic of life guide you towards your own unique and unforgettable ending.

Because just as a Bollywood film's ending lingers in our hearts and minds, so too should the story of your life leave a lasting impact on those around you. Let it be a story that inspires others to chase their own dreams, to embrace their individuality, and to create their own unique path in this world.

Remember, yaar, the ending of your story is not just about you. It's about the people you've touched, the lives you've impacted, and the legacy you leave behind. It's about inspiring others to embrace their own "Apna Time Aayega" and create a life that's filled with purpose, passion, and joy.

So, let your story be one that's worth telling, a story that's full of laughter, love, and unforgettable moments. Let it be a story that makes you proud, a story that makes you smile, a story that you'll cherish for years to come.

Just like a grand finale in a Bollywood film, your life's ending should leave a lasting impact. It's a culmination of all your experiences, relationships, and personal growth, echoing in the hearts and minds of those you've touched. It's a testament to the life you've lived, the love you've shared, and the dreams you've chased.

Imagine the final scene of your life's movie, yaar. It's not just about reaching a certain age or achieving specific goals. It's about the emotions you evoke, the memories you leave behind, and the inspiration you provide to others.

Are you surrounded by loved ones, their faces filled with gratitude for the joy and love you've brought into their lives? Do you see yourself looking back on a tapestry of experiences, rich with colors of adventure, compassion, and personal triumphs? Or perhaps you envision yourself passing on wisdom and knowledge, leaving behind a legacy that will continue to inspire generations to come.

Whatever your vision may be, make sure it's one that resonates with your soul, that reflects your values and aspirations. Create an ending that's not just satisfying, but deeply meaningful, leaving a lasting impact on the world around you.

Consider the story of a young woman named Amina, a talented artist from a conservative family in a small village. She dreams of showcasing her art to the world, of breaking free from the confines of tradition and pursuing her passion. But her family disapproves, urging her to focus on marriage and family instead.

Undeterred, Amina finds solace in her art, expressing her dreams and desires through vibrant colors and bold strokes. She paints in secret, hiding her canvases from prying eyes, and nurturing her talent in the quiet corners of her heart.

One day, a visiting tourist stumbles upon her hidden collection and is captivated by her raw talent and unique perspective. He encourages her to share her art with the world, and Amina, with newfound courage, decides to take a leap of faith.

She organizes a small exhibition in her village, showcasing her paintings to a skeptical audience. But as people gaze upon her vibrant canvases, they are moved by the emotions, the stories, and the dreams that Amina has poured into her art. Her work speaks to their hearts, transcending cultural barriers and societal expectations.

Amina's story is a testament to the power of following your dreams, even when the odds are stacked against you. It's a reminder that your ending is not predetermined by your circumstances or your background. It's a blank canvas, waiting for you to fill it with your own unique colors and strokes.

So, even if your path towards your Dalgona dream isn't a straight line, even if it's filled with twists and turns, detours and roadblocks, embrace the journey, my friend. Embrace the challenges, the setbacks, the moments of self-doubt. Because it's in those moments that you'll discover your true strength, your resilience, your ability to carve your own unique path in this world.

Remember, your story is still being written, yaar. The ending is not yet determined. It's up to you to fill those blank pages with your own unique colors, your own bold strokes.

So, pick up your pen, your paintbrush, your guitar, or whatever tool you choose to express yourself, and start creating your masterpiece. Embrace your individuality, celebrate your quirks, and let your light shine brightly.

Because your Dalgona dream is waiting, yaar. It's waiting for you to take that first step, to embrace the unknown, and to carve your own path to a fulfilling and joyful life.

And just like those iconic Bollywood dialogues that leave a lasting impression, let me leave you with this thought: "Aal izz well!" (All is well!). Because even amidst the chaos, the challenges, and the uncertainties, remember that you have the power to create your own happily ever after.

So, go on, yaar. Chase your dreams, embrace your journey, and let your story be a testament to the power of human spirit, the beauty of individuality, and the unwavering belief that you are in journey of becoming player 1 from player 456.

CHAPTER TEN

SIDE QUESTS: FINDING PASSION BEYOND THE GRIND

Picture this: You're stuck in the daily grind, clocking in and out, feeling like a cog in a giant machine. It's like being trapped in a never-ending game of "Red Light, Green Light," where you're constantly waiting for the green light to pursue your passions, but life keeps flashing red. You dream of exploring new horizons, of unleashing your creativity, of living a life that's more than just a paycheck.

But hey, don't worry, yaar. We've all been there. We've all felt the monotony of the 9-to-5, the yearning for something more, the desire to break free from the shackles of routine and embrace the extraordinary.

Remember that time your boss assigned you a mountain of paperwork on a Friday afternoon, just as you were about to head out for a weekend getaway with your friends? Or that time you had to cancel your dance class because of a last-minute meeting? It's enough to make you want to scream, "Zindagi sirf naukri nahin hai, yaar!" (Life is not just about work, dude!)

But here's the good news: even amidst the daily grind, you can still find pockets of joy, passion, and fulfillment. It's about discovering your "side quests," those little adventures that add spice and excitement to your life, that make you feel alive, that remind you that there's more to life than just work.

Think of it like those hidden levels in video games, where you stumble upon secret treasures, unlock new skills, and experience a whole new dimension of the game. Similarly, side quests in life can lead you to unexpected discoveries, hidden talents, and a renewed sense of purpose.

Just like Player 001, Oh Il-nam, the seemingly frail old man who joined the Squid Game not for the money, but for the thrill of reliving his childhood games and feeling alive again, we too can find joy and purpose in unexpected places. It might be volunteering at a local shelter, teaching kids how to play chess, or simply spending time with your grandparents, listening to their stories and soaking up their wisdom. These side quests might not pay the bills or boost your career, but they can enrich your life in ways that money can't buy.

Think about it, yaar. Life isn't just about climbing the corporate ladder or accumulating wealth. It's also about finding meaning and purpose in the things we do, the connections we make, and the experiences we have. It's about living a life that's not just successful, but also fulfilling and joyful.

So, the next time you're feeling stuck in the monotony of the daily grind, remember those hidden levels in video games, those secret treasures waiting to be discovered. Look for opportunities to explore new hobbies, to connect with like-minded people, to give back to your community.

It could be anything, yaar. Maybe it's learning how to play the guitar, joining a local sports team, or volunteering at an animal shelter. The important thing is to find something that ignites your passion, that makes your heart sing, that reminds you that there's more to life than just work.

Just like Ji-yeong, the young woman who formed a bond with Sae-byeok during the marble game, sometimes the most meaningful connections are made in the most unexpected places. They shared their stories, their dreams, and their vulnerabilities, finding solace and companionship in the midst of a brutal game.

Similarly, your side quests can lead you to meet amazing people, to form deep connections, and to build a community of support and encouragement. It might be a fellow volunteer at the local library, a teammate on your sports team, or a fellow enthusiast at a pottery class. These connections can enrich your life in ways you never imagined, providing you with a sense of belonging, purpose, and shared passion.

Think of those emotional scenes in "Schindler's List" where amidst the horrors of the Holocaust, Oskar Schindler finds redemption by saving the lives of countless Jews. He could have easily turned a blind eye, focused solely on his own profit and survival. But instead, he chose to act with compassion and humanity, risking his own safety to help others.

Similarly, your side quests can be a way to make a positive impact on the world, to contribute to something bigger than yourself, to leave a legacy that you can be proud of. It might be mentoring a young student, organizing a community cleanup drive, or simply lending a helping hand to someone in need.

These acts of kindness, these moments of compassion, can not only enrich the lives of others but also bring a deep sense of fulfillment and purpose to your own life. It's like adding a touch of soul to your existence, a reminder that you're not just a cog in a machine, but a human being with the power to make a difference.

So, yaar, don't underestimate the power of your side quests. They might not be as glamorous or as lucrative as your main job, but they can bring a sense of joy, purpose, and fulfillment that's priceless.

Think about your own life, yaar. Maybe you're a software engineer who secretly dreams of becoming a stand-up comedian, cracking jokes that would make even Kapil Sharma proud. Or perhaps you're a banker who finds solace in painting vibrant canvases, unleashing your inner Picasso after a long day of crunching numbers.

These hidden passions, these side quests, are not just distractions from your main job. They're a vital part of who you are, a source of joy, creativity, and fulfillment. They're like those secret spices that add flavor and depth to a dish, transforming it from ordinary to extraordinary.

So, don't be afraid to explore those hidden talents, yaar. Don't let your fears or insecurities hold you back. Give yourself permission to try new things, to step out of your comfort zone, and to see where your passions lead you.

Remember, life is too short to be stuck in a rut, doing the same thing day in and day out. It's about embracing the unexpected, the unknown, the unexplored. It's about finding those hidden gems, those side quests that make your heart sing and your soul soar.

Just like those hidden gems in the bylanes of Chandni Chowk, waiting to be discovered by the adventurous soul, your passions lie dormant, waiting for you to unlock them. They could be buried beneath the weight of responsibilities, drowned out by the noise of everyday life, or simply overshadowed by the fear of the unknown. But they are there, yaar, waiting for you to unleash them and let them shine.

Think of those hidden talents that emerge unexpectedly, like that shy accountant who secretly writes poetry that could rival Gulzar, or that reserved software engineer who strums a guitar like a rockstar on weekends. These side quests, these passions beyond the grind, are not just hobbies or distractions. They are a vital part of who you are, a source of joy, creativity, and fulfillment.

They are like those colorful spices that add flavor and depth to a dish, transforming it from bland and ordinary to something truly extraordinary. They are the secret ingredient that makes your life's recipe complete, adding that extra zing, that special touch that makes it uniquely yours.

Just remember the scene from squid game when Sang-woo discovered his knack for strategy during the Tug-of-War game, you too might surprise yourself with hidden talents or passions you never knew existed. Sang-woo, a man burdened by debt and desperation, revealed a sharp mind and a leadership quality that no one, not even himself, expected.

Similarly, your side quests might unlock hidden potentials, leading you down paths you never imagined. It's about giving yourself the chance to explore, to experiment, and to see what sparks your soul.

So, don't let the fear of the unknown or the pressure to conform to societal expectations hold you back. Embrace the "jugaad" spirit, take a leap of faith, and see where your side quests lead you.

Remember, the most fulfilling journeys are often the ones that take us off the beaten path and into uncharted territories. They're the ones that challenge us to grow, to learn, and to discover the hidden treasures that lie within us.

Think about your buddy, Kunal. A mild-mannered accountant by day, he secretly harbored a passion for stand-up comedy. Weekends would find him huddled in dimly-lit cafes, scribbling jokes on napkins, his heart pounding with a mix of excitement and fear. He'd practice his routines in front of the bathroom mirror, imagining the roar of the crowd, the spotlight shining on him.

One day, he mustered the courage to sign up for an open mic night at a local comedy club. The stage lights were blinding, his palms were sweaty, and his jokes felt like lead balloons in the tense silence. But Kunal, channeling his inner Russell Peters, soldiered on. He stumbled, he fumbled, but he also cracked a few jokes that elicited genuine laughter from the audience.

That night, Kunal didn't win any awards or become an overnight sensation. But he discovered something far more valuable - a sense of purpose, a passion that ignited his soul.

His side quest of stand-up comedy wasn't just a hobby; it was a lifeline, a way to express himself, to connect with others, and to bring laughter into the world.

Kunal's story is a testament to the power of pursuing your passions, even if they seem unconventional or impractical. It's about finding those hidden gems within yourself, those side quests that add color and vibrancy to your life.

So, the next time you feel that spark of curiosity, that urge to try something new, don't ignore it. Embrace it, nurture it, and see where it leads you. You might just discover a hidden talent, a newfound passion, or a whole new dimension of yourself that you never knew existed.

And it's not just about the big, flashy dreams, yaar. Sometimes, the most fulfilling side quests are the quiet, unassuming ones. Maybe it's volunteering at a local orphanage, where you discover the joy of bringing a smile to a child's face. Or maybe it's learning a new language, opening up a whole new world of literature, culture, and connections.

Perhaps it's simply taking the time to nurture a neglected garden, watching it bloom and flourish under your care, a testament to the power of patience and dedication.

These side quests might not make headlines or earn you a standing ovation, but they can fill your life with a quiet sense of purpose and satisfaction. They can remind you of the beauty that exists beyond the daily grind, the joy that can be found in the simplest of things.

So, yaar, don't underestimate the power of your side quests. They might just be the key to unlocking a hidden part of yourself, a passion that ignites your soul, a purpose that gives your life meaning.

Remember, life isn't just a series of tasks and responsibilities. It's a symphony of experiences, emotions, and connections. It's a dance between the mundane and the magical, the ordinary and the extraordinary.

And just like a Bollywood movie that blends laughter and tears, action and romance, your life too should be a tapestry of diverse experiences, a symphony of contrasting emotions, a journey that's as rich and fulfilling as your favorite masala chai.

So, in this grand tapestry of life, your side quests are the intricate patterns, the hidden details, the subtle nuances that add depth and richness to your story. They are the spices that make your dish flavorful, the unexpected harmonies that make your music soulful, the hidden brushstrokes that transform a blank canvas into a masterpiece.

They are the whispers of your soul, reminding you of the passions that lie dormant within you, the dreams that yearn to be fulfilled, and the possibilities that await you beyond the boundaries of the ordinary.

Just as the wise men and philosophers throughout history have sought meaning and purpose beyond the material world, so too must we venture beyond the confines of our daily routines to discover the true essence of our being.

It's in those moments of quiet contemplation, of introspection and self-discovery, that we truly connect with our inner selves, our passions, and our purpose. It's in those moments of creative expression, of selfless service, and of joyful pursuit of our hobbies that we find true fulfillment and contentment.

So, yaar, let's not just exist, let's truly live. Let's not just work, let's also play. Let's not just survive, let's thrive.

Embrace your side quests, my friend. Nurture your passions, explore your hidden talents, and let your spirit soar. Because in the grand symphony of life, it's the harmonious blend of work, play, and passion that creates a melody that's truly unforgettable.

Think about Player 067, Kang Sae-byeok, the North Korean defector who entered the Squid Game with a singular focus: to win enough money to reunite her family. But amidst the brutal competition and life-threatening challenges, she found moments of connection, compassion, and even love. She formed an unlikely bond with Ji-yeong, sharing stories, dreams, and vulnerabilities, and ultimately sacrificing her own chance at victory to give her friend a better shot at survival.

Sae-byeok's story reminds us that even in the most dire of circumstances, we can still find moments of beauty, connection, and meaning. It's about looking beyond the surface, recognizing the humanity in others, and extending a hand of friendship and compassion.

Similarly, your side quests can offer you opportunities to connect with others on a deeper level, to forge meaningful relationships, and to experience the joy of giving and receiving support. It might be volunteering at a local soup kitchen, mentoring a young student, or simply lending a listening ear to a friend in need. These seemingly small acts of kindness can have a ripple effect, not only brightening someone else's day but also bringing a sense of purpose and fulfillment to your own life.

So, yaar, don't let the pressures of the game, the relentless pursuit of success, or the fear of failure blind you to the beauty that surrounds you. Take a moment to appreciate the simple joys, the unexpected connections, and the heartwarming moments that make life worth living.

Just like Sae-byeok, who found solace and friendship in the most unlikely of places, you too can discover hidden treasures, unexpected joys, and deep connections in the most ordinary of circumstances.

Your side quests can be a way to express your creativity, explore your passions, and make a meaningful contribution to the world.

Whether it's volunteering at a local community center, mentoring a young student, or simply lending a helping hand to a neighbor in need, these acts of service can bring a sense of purpose and fulfillment that transcends the daily grind.

Remember, yaar, life is not just about what you achieve for yourself, but also about the impact you make on the lives of others. It's about spreading kindness, sharing your talents, and contributing to the greater good.

Just like those heartwarming Bollywood scenes where the hero selflessly helps others, your side quests can be a way to showcase your own humanity, compassion, and generosity. They can be a reminder that even the smallest acts of kindness can have a ripple effect, creating a positive impact that extends far beyond your own immediate circle.

So, yaar, don't underestimate the power of your side quests. They might not bring you fame or fortune, but they can bring you something far more valuable - a sense of purpose, a feeling of connection, and the satisfaction of knowing that you're making a difference in the world.

Embrace them, nurture them, and let them be a source of joy, inspiration, and fulfillment in your life. Because just like those hidden gems in the bylanes of your city, your side quests might just be the key to unlocking a whole new world of possibilities, a world where you can truly shine and make your mark.

Just like a skilled potter molding clay on a spinning wheel, you too have the power to shape and mold your life into a work of art. It may take time, effort, and a few misshapen pots along the way, but with patience, perseverance, and a touch of "jugaad," you can create something truly beautiful and unique.

Remember, your Dalgona dream isn't just about the end result, it's about the process, the journey, the transformation that takes place within you as you pursue your passions and overcome challenges. It's about discovering hidden talents, building resilience, and finding joy in the pursuit of something that truly matters to you.

So, embrace the messiness, the imperfections, and the unexpected twists and turns along the way. Remember, even the most skilled potter starts with a lump of clay, and it's through their hands, their vision, and their dedication that it transforms into a work of art.

Similarly, your life is a blank canvas, waiting for you to paint your own masterpiece. It's up to you to choose the colors, the brushstrokes, and the composition. It's up to you to create a story that's both meaningful and memorable.

So, let your creativity flow. Let your passion guide you. Let your dreams soar. And remember, just like those stunning pieces of pottery that adorn our homes and museums, your life too can be a work of art, a testament to the beauty, resilience, and infinite possibilities of the human spirit.

Just like a skilled musician who practices their instrument day in and day out, honing their skills and mastering their craft, you too need to nurture your passions and talents. It's about dedicating time and effort to the things that ignite your soul, that make you feel alive, that bring you a sense of joy and fulfillment.

Remember, your side quests are not just distractions or hobbies; they are an integral part of who you are. They are the melodies that make your heart sing, the rhythms that move your soul, the harmonies that create a symphony of purpose and meaning in your life.

So, practice your craft, yaar. Whether it's playing the guitar, writing poetry, painting, or simply spending time in nature, dedicate yourself to the things that bring you joy. Don't let the pressures of the world, the demands of your job, or the expectations of others stifle your creativity or dampen your spirit.

Just like those legendary musicians who have touched our hearts and inspired us with their melodies, you too have the power to create your own music, your own unique sound that resonates with the world.

So, let your passion be your guide, your creativity your compass, and your joy your fuel. Embrace your side quests, nurture your talents, and let your spirit soar. Because when you do what you love, when you pursue your passions with unwavering dedication, you create a life that's not just successful, but also deeply fulfilling and meaningful.

And remember, yaar, just like a beautiful melody that lingers in our ears long after the music stops, the impact of your side quests will resonate far beyond your own life. It will inspire others, uplift those around you, and create a legacy that's worth remembering.

So, go on, my friend. Pick up that instrument, that paintbrush, that pen, or whatever tool you choose to express yourself. And let the world witness the magic that unfolds when you embrace your passions and carve your own unique path in this grand symphony called life.

CHAPTER ELEVEN

IMPOSTER SYNDROME: YOU'RE NOT A SQUARE

Imagine yourself, standing at the gates of a fancy-dress party. Everyone's dressed to the nines, sporting elaborate costumes and masks that hide their true identities. You, on the other hand, feel like you're wearing a cardboard box with a smiley face drawn on it. You're surrounded by confident, charismatic individuals who seem to know exactly who they are and what they want, while you're struggling to even recognize your own reflection in the mirror.

Welcome to the Imposter Syndrome party, my friend, where everyone seems to be a shape-shifting master of disguise, except you. It's a place where self-doubt reigns supreme, where that nagging voice in your head whispers, "You don't belong here. You're not good enough. You're just faking it till you make it."

It's like that time you got invited to a high-profile business conference, surrounded by CEOs, entrepreneurs, and industry leaders. You felt like a fish out of water, your imposter syndrome screaming louder than a Bollywood item song. You questioned your qualifications, your achievements, even your right to be in the same room as these seemingly successful individuals.

But here's the thing, imposter syndrome is a universal struggle. Even the most accomplished individuals, from Oscar-winning actors to Nobel laureates, have experienced that nagging feeling of self-doubt, that fear of being exposed as a fraud.

It's like those villains who masquerade as heroes, fooling everyone with their charm and charisma, until their true intentions are revealed. Similarly, imposter syndrome can make us feel like we're constantly putting on a show, hiding our insecurities and vulnerabilities behind a mask of confidence.

But just like those heroes who eventually unmask the villain and expose their true colors, we too can overcome imposter syndrome by recognizing its presence and challenging its lies. It's about acknowledging our achievements, embracing our strengths, and recognizing that we are worthy of our success, no matter what our inner critic might say.

Think about Player 212, Han Mi-nyeo, the loud-mouthed, brash woman who seemed to bulldoze her way through the games, using manipulation and deceit to get ahead. She projected an image of confidence and self-assurance, but beneath the surface, she was deeply insecure, craving acceptance and validation.

Just like Mi-nyeo, we often try to mask our insecurities with bravado, projecting an image of competence and success, even when we feel like we're barely keeping it together. We fear that if people see our true selves, our flaws and vulnerabilities, they'll reject us, judge us, or deem us unworthy.

But here's the thing, yaar: vulnerability is not a weakness, it's a strength. It's what makes us human, it's what allows us to connect with others on a deeper level, and it's what ultimately allows us to overcome imposter syndrome.

Just like Mi-nyeo, who eventually found solace and companionship in the most unexpected of places, we too can find strength in our vulnerabilities. We can learn to embrace our imperfections, to acknowledge our fears, and to share our struggles with those we trust.

It's about recognizing that we're all in this together, that everyone has their own insecurities and self-doubts, and that it's okay to not have all the answers. It's about letting go of the need to be perfect and embracing the beautiful mess that is our true selves.

Imagine, if you will, that your brain is a bustling marketplace, a Chandni Chowk of thoughts and emotions. Amidst the vibrant chaos, there's a tiny stall tucked away in a corner, manned by a grumpy old shopkeeper named Imposter Syndrome. He's got a knack for selling you defective goods, convincing you that your achievements are mere flukes, your talents are insignificant, and your success is undeserved.

He'll whisper In your ear, "Arre bhai, you got lucky this time. Next time, your true colors will be exposed. You're just a fraud, a pretender, a wannabe." And before you know it, you're haggling with him, trying to convince yourself that you're not as bad as he makes you out to be.

But here's the thing, yaar: Imposter Syndrome is a master salesman, a smooth talker who knows how to play on your insecurities. He'll use your past failures, your perceived shortcomings, and even your successes against you. He'll make you believe that you're not worthy of your achievements, that you're just one step away from being exposed as a fraud.

But just like those savvy shoppers in Chandni Chowk who know how to spot a fake, you too can learn to recognize the tricks of Imposter Syndrome and refuse to buy into his lies. It's about developing a discerning eye, a critical mind, and a healthy dose of self-belief.

It's about reminding yourself that you're not defined by your mistakes or your failures. You're defined by your resilience, your perseverance, and your unwavering determination to succeed. You're defined by the countless hours you've spent honing your skills, the sacrifices you've made, and the obstacles you've overcome.

So, the next time Imposter Syndrome tries to sell you his defective goods, tell him to take a hike, yaar. Remind him that you're not a gullible tourist, you're a seasoned shopper who knows the value of your own worth. You're not a fraud, a pretender, or a wannabe. You're a capable, talented, and deserving individual who's earned their place in the world.

Remember our friend, Priya? The one who's always doubting herself, even though she's a whiz at coding and can whip up a website faster than you can say "chai latte"? She landed a dream job at a top tech company, but instead of celebrating, she was convinced she'd be exposed as a fraud.

Every time she solved a complex coding problem, she'd think, "Phew, I got lucky this time." Every compliment from her boss was met with a mental shrug, "They don't really know how clueless I am sometimes."

It was like she was constantly playing a game of hide-and-seek with her own confidence, always expecting to be found out. But one day, during a team meeting, Priya's boss praised her innovative solution to a particularly tricky bug.

Instead of brushing it off, Priya took a deep breath and said, "Thank you. I worked really hard on that, and I'm proud of the result."

It was a small victory, but it was a turning point. Priya realized that she wasn't a fraud, she was a talented coder who deserved to be there. She started to own her accomplishments, to speak up more confidently in meetings, and to embrace her own unique brand of brilliance.

Priya's story is a reminder that imposter syndrome can strike anyone, even the most capable and accomplished individuals. But it's not a life sentence, yaar. It's a battle that can be won, one small victory at a time.

So, the next time you find yourself doubting your abilities, remember Priya's story. Remember that you're not alone, that everyone feels like an imposter sometimes. But also remember that you have the power to challenge those negative thoughts, to embrace your strengths, and to celebrate your successes.

Just like Cho Sang-woo, the brilliant strategist who seemed to have it all figured out, we too can fall into the trap of believing that our achievements are solely based on luck or external factors. Sang-woo's sharp mind and analytical skills propelled him through the games, but his underlying insecurities and fear of failure led him down a dark path of manipulation and betrayal.

Similarly, we often attribute our successes to external factors, downplaying our own hard work, talent, and dedication. We might think, "I only got this job because I knew someone," or "I aced that exam because it was easy." We fail to recognize our own contributions, our own unique skills and abilities that have led us to where we are today.

But just as Sang-woo's downfall was ultimately caused by his inability to acknowledge his own worth and embrace his vulnerabilities, so too can our own self-doubt and imposter syndrome sabotage our success and happiness.

It's time to break free from this cycle, yaar. It's time to recognize that you are not a fraud, a pretender, or a lucky charm. You are a capable, talented, and deserving individual who has earned their place in the world.

Just like those players in the Squid Game who eventually realized the importance of teamwork and collaboration, we too need to build a support system, a tribe of people who believe in us and remind us of our worth.

Surround yourself with positive influences, yaar. Seek out mentors, friends, and family members who will uplift you, encourage you, and challenge you to grow. Share your fears and insecurities with them, and let them remind you of your strengths and accomplishments.

Remember, you're not alone in this battle against imposter syndrome. We all have our moments of self-doubt, but with the right support system and a healthy dose of self-compassion, we can overcome those doubts and embrace our true selves.

But hey, we're not talking rocket science here. Overcoming imposter syndrome is like mastering that tricky dance step in a Saroj Khan choreography – it takes practice, patience, and a whole lot of self-belief.

So, how do you kick imposter syndrome to the curb and unleash your inner superstar? Let's break it down, Bollywood ishtyle:

* Face Your Fears, Like a DDLJ Climax: Remember that scene where Raj finally confronts Bauji and declares his love for Simran? It's time to channel your inner Raj and confront your imposter syndrome head-on. Acknowledge those nagging doubts, those whispers of inadequacy, and then challenge them with a resounding "Bade bade deshon mein aisi choti choti baatein hoti rehti hain, Senorita!" (In big countries, such small things happen all the time, Senorita!). Remind yourself of your accomplishments, your strengths, and the unique value you bring to the table.

* Celebrate Your Wins, Like a Big Fat Indian Wedding: Don't be shy to pat yourself on the back, yaar! Every achievement, big or small, deserves a celebration. Did you finally finish that project you've been procrastinating on? Did you learn a new skill? Did you simply make it through a tough day with a smile on your face? Break out the dhol, put on your dancing shoes, and celebrate your wins, Bollywood ishtyle!

* Build Your Tribe, Like the "Zindagi Na Milegi Dobara" Gang: Surround yourself with people who lift you up, who believe in you, and who remind you of your worth. Just like those three friends who embarked on a life-changing road trip, find your own tribe of supporters who will cheer you on, challenge you to grow, and remind you that you're not alone in this journey.

* Embrace Your Quirks, Like a Govinda Dance Move: Don't try to fit into a mold that doesn't suit you, yaar. Embrace your quirks, your unique personality, your own brand of masala. Just like Govinda's iconic dance moves that defied convention and brought a smile to our faces,

let your individuality shine through. Remember, it's your quirks that make you special, that make you stand out from the crowd.

* Practice Self-Compassion, Like a Warm Hug from Your Mom: We all make mistakes, yaar. We all have bad days. We all stumble and fall sometimes. But instead of beating yourself up, treat yourself with kindness and understanding. Just like your mom's warm embrace that can melt away all your worries, practice self-compassion and remind yourself that you're doing the best you can.

Remember, self-compassion is like that soothing balm your mom applies on your wounds, a gentle reminder that it's okay to feel hurt, to make mistakes, and to need a little extra care sometimes.

It's about offering yourself the same kindness and understanding that you would offer to a dear friend, rather than berating yourself with harsh self-criticism.

So, the next time you find yourself feeling like an imposter, like you don't deserve your success or your happiness, try to counter those thoughts with a dose of self-compassion. Remind yourself that you're not alone, that everyone struggles with self-doubt at times, and that it's okay to not be perfect.

And just like those underdog heroes in Bollywood movies who always find a way to overcome their challenges, you too have the strength and resilience to conquer imposter syndrome.

It might take time, effort, and a whole lot of self-love, but with the right mindset and a supportive tribe by your side, you can silence that inner critic and embrace your true self, flaws and all.

Because remember, yaar, you're not a square peg trying to fit into a round hole. You're a unique, multifaceted individual with your own special talents and abilities. And the world needs your authenticity, your creativity, and your passion.

So, don't let imposter syndrome dim your light. Shine brightly, my friend, and let the world see the amazing person that you are.

Let's take a trip down memory lane, back to our college days, shall we? Remember our friend, the one and only "Rocket" Rahul? This guy was a legend, a master of jugaad, and a walking encyclopedia of Bollywood trivia. He could recite dialogues from "Sholay" faster than Gabbar Singh could count his men, and his dance moves could rival any Govinda performance.

But Rahul's biggest talent was his ability to turn any mundane situation into a hilarious adventure. Like that time during our final exams when he convinced the entire hostel to stage a midnight protest against the mess food, complete with slogans, placards, and even a makeshift dhol-tasha band.

Or that time he disguised himself as a professor and delivered a lecture on the "Importance of Jugaad in Engineering," leaving the actual professor speechless and the entire class in stitches.

Rahul's antics might have landed us in trouble with the authorities a few times, but they also taught us valuable lessons about embracing our creativity, finding joy in the everyday, and never taking life too seriously.

He showed us that even amidst the stress of exams, the pressure of deadlines, and the monotony of college life, there's always room for laughter, for adventure, and for creating memories that will last a lifetime.

So, the next time you find yourself feeling overwhelmed by the challenges of life, remember Rahul and his infectious spirit. Remember that laughter is the best medicine, that a little bit of mischief can go a long way, and that sometimes, the most valuable lessons are learned not in the classroom, but in the spontaneous moments of joy and camaraderie.

Embrace your inner Rahul, yaar. Let your creativity flow, your humor shine, and your spirit soar. Because life is too short to be taken too seriously. It's a game, a dance, a celebration. So, go out there and play, dance, and celebrate, with the same gusto and enthusiasm that Rahul brought to our college days.

But let's not forget, yaar, that self-love isn't just about acceptance, it's also about growth. It's about pushing yourself beyond your comfort zone, challenging your limits, and striving to become the best version of yourself.

Just like those Bollywood heroes who undergo rigorous training montages to prepare for the final showdown, you too need to invest in your own personal growth and development. It might mean learning a new skill, taking up a new hobby, or simply reading a book that expands your horizons.

Remember, self-love isn't about stagnation, it's about evolution. It's about constantly striving to improve yourself, to learn new things, to become a wiser, kinder, and more compassionate human being.

Think of it like tending to a garden, where you water the plants, prune the branches, and nurture the soil to ensure its growth and vitality. Similarly, self-love requires constant attention and care. It's about feeding your mind with positive thoughts, your body with nourishing food, and your soul with meaningful experiences.

So, invest in yourself, yaar. Take the time to learn, to grow, to evolve. Embrace challenges, seek out opportunities, and never stop pushing yourself to reach new heights. Because just like a well-tended garden that blooms with vibrant colors and fragrant scents, a life filled with self-love and personal growth is a beautiful thing to behold.

Remember that pivotal moment in the Squid Game when the players had a choice: to continue playing the deadly games or to vote and walk away. It was a test of their courage, their resilience, and their willingness to stand up for what they believed in.

Similarly, in the game of life, we too face choices that can either lead us closer to our dreams or trap us in a cycle of fear and self-doubt. It takes courage to step outside our comfort zones, to challenge the status quo, and to pursue our passions, even when the odds seem stacked against us.

Just like those players who chose to walk away from the game, recognizing the value of their own lives and the importance of human connection, we too need to make choices that align with our values and priorities. It's about saying no to toxic relationships, to dead-end jobs, to anything that diminishes our self-worth or hinders our growth.

It's about saying yes to opportunities that challenge us, that inspire us, and that bring us closer to our Dalgona dreams. It's about choosing our own path, even if it means going against the grain, even if it means facing criticism or rejection.

Because in the end, yaar, it's not about winning or losing. It's about playing the game of life with integrity, compassion, and an unwavering belief in yourself. It's about creating an ending that you're proud of, a story that reflects your true self, your passions, and your dreams.

So, the next time you find yourself at a crossroads, facing a difficult choice, remember those brave players who dared to walk away from the Squid Game. Remember that you too have the power to choose your own path, to create your own ending, to live a life that's truly yours.

And just like those unforgettable moments in the Squid Game that taught us about the resilience of the human spirit, the importance of friendship, and the power of hope, let your life be a testament to the same values.

Let it be a story of courage, compassion, and unwavering self-belief. Because in the end, yaar, that's what truly matters. It's not about the games we play, but the choices we make, the connections we forge, and the impact we leave on the world.

Think about Che Guevara, the iconic revolutionary who famously abandoned his medical career and comfortable life to fight for social justice and equality in Latin America. It wasn't the lure of fame or fortune that drove him, but a deep sense of purpose and a burning desire to make a difference in the world.

Imagine young Ernesto "Che" Guevara, a medical student with a promising future, suddenly deciding to embark on a motorcycle journey across South America with his friend Alberto Granado. They witnessed poverty, injustice, and exploitation, and Che's heart ached for the marginalized and oppressed.

Legend has it that during their travels, Che and Alberto ran out of money and resorted to some rather unconventional methods to survive. In one particularly hilarious incident, they tried to barter their medical skills for a meal at a local restaurant. The owner, unimpressed by their offer to treat his indigestion, politely declined, leaving the two adventurers hungry but amused.

This story, while lighthearted, reveals Che's unwavering commitment to his ideals, his willingness to step outside his comfort zone, and his ability to find humor even in the most challenging of situations. He didn't let societal expectations or the pursuit of material wealth dictate his path. Instead, he chose to follow his heart, to fight for what he believed in, and to create a life that was meaningful and impactful.

Che Guevara's story is a powerful reminder that our side quests, our passions beyond the grind, can lead us to extraordinary destinations. They can ignite our souls, challenge our perspectives, and ultimately shape the course of our lives.

So, what's the takeaway, yaar? It's simple: your side quests aren't just a way to escape the daily grind, they're a pathway to a richer, more fulfilling life. They're a chance to discover hidden talents, to forge meaningful connections, to make a difference in the world, and to ultimately become the best version of yourself.

Just like our favorite Bollywood movies, your life is a story waiting to be told. It's a canvas waiting to be painted, a symphony waiting to be composed, a dance waiting to be performed. And your side quests, my friend, are the colorful threads that weave together the tapestry of your life, adding depth, texture, and vibrancy to your story.

So, don't be afraid to step off the beaten path, yaar. Don't be afraid to explore the unknown, to embrace the unexpected, to follow your passions wherever they may lead. Because in the end, it's not just about the destination, it's about the journey. And it's up to you to make it a journey that's worth remembering.

Think about the quiet strength of Player 001, Oh Il-nam, the elderly man who initially seemed frail and vulnerable. He might not have had the physical prowess of the younger contestants, but he possessed a wisdom and resilience that transcended the game itself.

Remember his simple strategy during the "Ddakji" game? He didn't try to overpower his opponents with brute force; instead, he used his knowledge of human psychology to gain their trust and cooperation. He reminded us that success isn't always about physical strength or brute force; it's about using your mind, your heart, and your unique skills to navigate challenges and achieve your goals.

Just like Il-nam, who found joy in the simple act of playing games and connecting with others, we too can find fulfillment in the pursuit of our passions, regardless of our age, background, or perceived limitations. It's about embracing our inner child, rekindling that spark of curiosity, and finding joy in the simple pleasures of life.

So, the next time you feel like you're too old, too inexperienced, or too unqualified to pursue your dreams, remember Il-nam's gentle smile and unwavering spirit. Remember that age is just a number, that experience is overrated, and that passion knows no bounds.

Embrace your inner child, yaar. Let your curiosity guide you, your creativity inspire you, and your joy fuel your journey. Because just like Il-nam, who found a sense of purpose and belonging in the most unexpected of places, you too can discover a world of possibilities when you dare to step outside your comfort zone and embrace the unknown.

And just like those side characters in Bollywood films, the ones who often steal the show with their wit, charm, and unwavering support for the protagonist, your chosen tribe can also play a crucial role in helping you overcome imposter syndrome.

They are your cheerleaders, your confidantes, your sounding boards. They are the ones who remind you of your strengths, celebrate your achievements, and offer a listening ear when you're feeling overwhelmed by self-doubt.

Think of those heartwarming scenes in "Dil Chahta Hai" where Akash, Sameer, and Sid support each other through heartbreak, career challenges, and personal growth. They remind us that true friendship is about being there for each other, through thick and thin, offering a safe space to express our fears, doubts, and vulnerabilities.

Similarly, your tribe can provide that safe space for you, a place where you can be yourself, without judgment or criticism. They can help you reframe your negative thoughts, remind you of your accomplishments, and celebrate your wins, big or small.

But it's not just about receiving support, yaar. It's also about giving it. Just like those unsung heroes in Bollywood movies, the ones who quietly contribute to the success of the protagonist, you too can play a crucial role in the lives of your friends and loved ones.

Be their cheerleader, their confidante, their shoulder to lean on. Offer them your support, your encouragement, and your unwavering belief in their abilities. By lifting others up, you'll also be lifting yourself up, reminding yourself of your own worth and the positive impact you can have on the world.

Remember, yaar, we're all in this together. We all have our own struggles, our own insecurities, our own battles with imposter syndrome. But by creating a supportive and empowering community, we can help each other overcome these challenges and achieve our full potential.

So, the next time you find yourself feeling like an imposter, remember the power of your tribe. Reach out to your friends, your family, your mentors, and let them remind you of your worth. Share your fears and doubts with them, and allow them to offer you the love, support, and encouragement you need to overcome those feelings.

Because just like those Bollywood movies that teach us the importance of friendship, love, and community, your tribe can be the key to unlocking your true potential and silencing that pesky imposter syndrome once and for all.

But how do you do it? Well, it all starts with recognizing the signs of imposter syndrome. Do you often feel like a fraud, even when you've achieved success? Do you attribute your accomplishments to luck or external factors, rather than your own hard work and talent? Do you constantly compare yourself to others, feeling inadequate and unworthy?

If you answered yes to any of these questions, then you might be experiencing imposter syndrome. But don't worry, yaar, you're not alone. It's a common struggle, even among the most successful and accomplished individuals.

The key to overcoming imposter syndrome is to challenge those negative thoughts and beliefs. It's about reframing your perspective, recognizing your own worth, and celebrating your achievements, no matter how big or small.

Just like those underdog heroes in Bollywood movies who rise above their circumstances and prove their naysayers wrong, you too have the power to silence that inner critic and embrace your true potential.

So, the next time you find yourself doubting your abilities or feeling like a fraud, remember that you're not alone. Remember that everyone struggles with self-doubt at times, even the most successful and accomplished individuals.

But also remember that you have the power to change the narrative. You have the power to rewrite your story, to challenge those negative thoughts, and to embrace your own unique brand of brilliance.

So, take a deep breath, yaar, and look in the mirror. See the reflection of a strong, capable, and deserving individual who's ready to take on the world.

Because you're not a square peg trying to fit into a round hole. You're a unique, multifaceted gem, shining brightly in your own way. And the world needs your light, your passion, your authenticity.

So, let go of the imposter syndrome, my friend. Embrace your true self, flaws and all. Because you are worthy, you are enough, and you are destined for greatness.

And remember, just like those iconic Bollywood dialogues that leave a lasting impression, let this be your mantra: "Main apni favourite hoon!" (I am my own favorite!).

Because, yaar, that's the ultimate truth. And the sooner you believe it, the sooner you'll start living a life that's truly yours, a life that's filled with joy, purpose, and unapologetic self-love.

CHAPTER TWELVE

LEVELING UP: SKILLS FOR REAL-LIFE WINS

Life's Not a Video Game, But You Can Still Cheat Code Your Way to Success!

Picture this, yaar: You're stuck in a level of your favorite video game, battling fierce enemies, dodging obstacles, and desperately searching for that elusive power-up that will give you an edge. You've tried every trick in the book, but nothing seems to work. You're on the verge of giving up, when suddenly, you stumble upon a hidden cheat code that unlocks a whole new world of possibilities.

It's like that time you were struggling to solve a complex coding problem, pulling your hair out in frustration, when your friend whispered a secret shortcut that made everything click. Or that time you were trying to impress your crush with your culinary skills, when your mom shared her secret recipe for the perfect biryani.

Welcome to Chapter 13, my friend, where we'll explore the art of leveling up in real life, of finding those "cheat codes" that can give you an edge, help you overcome challenges, and achieve your goals.

But hold on, yaar, before you start searching for a magic lamp or a genie in a bottle, let me assure you that this isn't about finding shortcuts or taking the easy way out. It's about discovering the tools, strategies, and skills that can help you navigate life's challenges with confidence, resilience, and a whole lot of jugaad.

Think of it like those life hacks you see on YouTube, those clever tricks that make everyday tasks easier, faster, and more efficient. It's about finding those little shortcuts, those hidden gems of wisdom that can help you unlock your full potential and achieve your dreams.

But hey, this ain't just about saving time or money, yaar. It's about investing in yourself, developing your skills, and becoming the best version of yourself. It's about leveling up your game, both personally and professionally, so that you can tackle any challenge that comes your way.

Think about our buddy, Ankit. An unassuming IT professional during the week, his weekends were transformed into a vibrant canvas of laughter and applause. In dimly-lit cafes, his pen danced across notepads, scribbling jokes that tickled the funny bone. He'd rehearse his routines in front of the bathroom mirror, his reflection morphing into a confident stand-up comedian under the imaginary spotlight.

One fateful evening, he stepped onto the stage of a local comedy club, his heart pounding louder than the dhol beats of a Punjabi wedding. The stage lights were unforgiving, exposing his nervous jitters, and the initial silence from the audience felt heavier than a sack of potatoes. But Ankit, channeling his inner Zakir Khan, persevered. His jokes might have stumbled at first, but soon, they found their rhythm, hitting the bullseye of the audience's humor, eliciting genuine laughter and applause.

That night, Ankit might not have won any awards, but he discovered a treasure chest within himself – a passion that set his soul on fire. His "side quest" of stand-up comedy wasn't merely a hobby; it was his escape, his creative outlet, and a source of pure, unadulterated joy.

Ankit's tale reminds us that the most fulfilling side quests are often the ones we least expect. They're the hidden talents waiting to be unearthed, the passions yearning to be expressed, the dreams begging to be chased.

So, the next time you feel that spark of curiosity, that urge to try something new, don't dismiss it as a mere distraction. Embrace it, nurture it, and see where it leads you. You might just discover a hidden talent, a newfound passion, or a whole new dimension of yourself that you never knew existed.

But hey, leveling up isn't just about discovering hidden talents or pursuing creative passions. It's also about acquiring practical skills that can help you navigate the complexities of life, just like those cheat codes that unlock secret levels and hidden treasures in video games.

Think of it like learning how to cook a delicious meal, fix a leaky faucet, or negotiate a better salary. These skills might not seem as glamorous as playing the guitar or performing on stage, but they can empower you, boost your confidence, and make you feel more capable and self-sufficient.

Remember that time your friend's car broke down in the middle of nowhere, and you, armed with your trusty toolkit and a few YouTube tutorials, managed to fix it like a pro? Or that time you haggled with a street vendor and scored a bargain that would make even the most seasoned shopper proud?

These are the real-life wins, yaar, the moments when you realize that you're not just a passive observer, but an active participant in the game of life. It's about taking charge of your own destiny, equipping yourself with the skills and knowledge you need to thrive, and never shying away from a challenge.

So, the next time you encounter a problem, a hurdle, or a seemingly impossible task, don't panic. Instead, channel your inner jugaadu, tap into your resourcefulness, and find a creative solution. Remember, every challenge is an opportunity to learn, to grow, and to level up your game.

And just like those video game characters who gain experience points and unlock new abilities as they progress through the levels, you too can level up in real life by constantly learning, adapting, and evolving. It's about embracing a growth mindset, believing in your ability to improve, and never settling for mediocrity.

Remember the glass bridge game, where players had to choose between two seemingly identical panels, one tempered, one brittle? The fear of making the wrong choice, the uncertainty of each step, the constant threat of falling into oblivion – it mirrored the risks we take in life when pursuing our dreams.

Just like those players who carefully analyzed each panel, relying on their intuition and the faintest of clues, we too need to make calculated decisions, weigh our options, and trust our gut feelings. The path to our Dalgona dreams might not always be clear, but with careful consideration and a willingness to take risks, we can navigate the uncertainties and emerge victorious.

And even if we stumble, even if we make the wrong choice, remember that failure is not the end. It's a chance to learn, to recalibrate, and to find a new path forward. Just like those players who fell through the glass, we too might experience setbacks and disappointments. But it's our ability to pick ourselves up, dust ourselves off, and keep moving forward that truly defines us.

So, yaar, don't let the fear of failure paralyze you. Don't let the uncertainty of the future hold you back. Embrace the challenges, take those calculated risks, and trust your instincts.

Remember, every step you take, every decision you make, is a brushstroke on the canvas of your life. And with every stroke, you're creating a masterpiece that's uniquely yours, a testament to your courage, your resilience, and your unwavering pursuit of your Dalgona dreams.

But just as every Bollywood film needs a climax, your life's journey needs a grand finale, a satisfying resolution that ties all the threads together. It's the moment where you look back on your choices, your struggles, your triumphs, and feel a sense of peace and fulfillment. It's the scene where the hero finally defeats the villain, the lovers reunite, and the underdog achieves their dreams.

Your ending, just like a Bollywood ending, should be a celebration of your unique journey, a testament to your resilience, your courage, and your unwavering spirit. It should be a reminder that even in the face of adversity, you found the strength to carve your own path, to follow your dreams, and to live a life that's truly yours.

So, as you approach the final act of your life's movie, remember that you hold the pen. You are the director, the screenwriter, and the star of your own show. And just like those unforgettable Bollywood movies that leave us with a sense of hope and inspiration, let your story be one that's filled with love, laughter, and the unwavering belief that apna time aayega!

Because in the end, yaar, it's not about the destination, it's about the journey. It's about the people you meet, the experiences you have, and the lessons you learn along the way. It's about embracing the ups and downs, the twists and turns, and the unexpected detours that make life so unpredictable and so beautiful.

So, live your life to the fullest, my friend. Chase your dreams, embrace your passions, and surround yourself with people who lift you up and inspire you to be the best version of yourself.

And when the final credits roll, let your story be one that you're proud of, a story that leaves a lasting legacy, a story that says, "I lived my life on my own terms, I followed my heart, and I made a difference in the world."

So, even if your path towards your Dalgona dream isn't a straight line, even if it's filled with twists and turns, detours, and roadblocks, embrace the journey, my friend. Embrace the challenges, the setbacks, the moments of self-doubt. Because it's in those moments that you'll discover your true strength, your resilience, and your ability to carve your own unique path in this world.

Remember, your story is still being written. The ending is not yet determined. It's up to you to fill those blank pages with your own unique colors, your own bold strokes.

Remember our buddy, the one and only Raju Rastogi, the anxiety-ridden engineering student from "3 Idiots?" He was so terrified of exams and placements that he'd break out in a cold sweat at the mere mention of the word "interview." He'd spend sleepless nights cramming formulas and equations, convinced that his future depended on those three little letters: CGPA.

But one fateful day, Raju's fear reached its peak. On the morning of his placement interview, he locked himself in the bathroom, refusing to come out. It took all of Rancho's charm and Farhan's wit to coax him out, reminding him that life is more than just grades and job offers.

In a moment of desperation, they decided to take a drastic step. They shaved Raju's head, hoping that the shock of his new look would jolt him out of his anxiety spiral. And guess what? It worked! Raju, bald and bewildered, faced the interview panel with a newfound sense of confidence. He realized that his worth wasn't defined by his grades or his job prospects, but by his character, his resilience, and his ability to laugh at himself.

Raju's story is a reminder that sometimes, the most unexpected solutions can be the most effective. It's about finding your own unique "jugaad" to overcome challenges, to break free from self-limiting beliefs, and to embrace the absurdity of life.

So, the next time you find yourself facing a daunting task or feeling overwhelmed by anxiety, remember Raju's bald head and his newfound confidence. Remember that laughter can be a powerful weapon against fear, that sometimes, the most unconventional solutions can lead to the most surprising breakthroughs.

Embrace the absurdity of life, yaar. Find the humor in your struggles, the joy in the unexpected, and the resilience to keep going, even when things get tough. Because just like Raju, who eventually landed a job on his own terms, you too have the power to create your own happy ending, your own unique brand of success.

Think about that one friend we all have, the one who always seems to have it all together. They ace their exams without breaking a sweat, land their dream jobs effortlessly, and seem to glide through life with a smile that could light up a Diwali night.

But one evening, over a cup of chai and a plate of pakoras, that friend confides in you. They reveal the anxieties that plague them, the self-doubts that gnaw at their confidence, the fear that they're not truly living up to their potential.

It's a moment of vulnerability, a glimpse into the hidden struggles that even the most seemingly successful people face. It's a reminder that we all wear masks, that we all have our own battles to fight, our own demons to conquer.

In that moment, you realize that your friend, just like you, is on a journey of self-discovery, navigating the complexities of life with both courage and trepidation. They might have achieved external success, but they're still searching for that inner peace, that sense of belonging, that feeling of truly being enough.

It's a powerful reminder that we're all in this together, yaar. We all have our own struggles, our own insecurities, our own battles to fight. But by sharing our vulnerabilities, by supporting each other, and by celebrating our unique journeys, we can create a community of love, acceptance, and understanding.

So, the next time you find yourself comparing your life to others, remember that everyone has their own hidden struggles. Remember that success isn't just about external achievements, it's also about inner peace and fulfillment. And remember that true friendship is about being there for each other, through the good times and the bad, offering a shoulder to lean on and a listening ear.

Remember, life is not a spectator sport. It's a game where you're the player, the strategist, and the champion. It's up to you to identify your strengths, weaknesses, and areas for improvement. It's up to you to seek out the knowledge, skills, and resources that will help you level up your game.

Think of it like training for a marathon. You wouldn't just show up on race day expecting to win, would you? You'd need to put in the miles, train your body, and develop a strategy to pace yourself and reach the finish line.

Similarly, achieving your goals in life requires preparation, dedication, and a willingness to push your limits. It's about setting clear objectives, breaking them down into smaller, achievable steps, and then taking consistent action towards those goals.

But just like a marathon runner who faces moments of fatigue, self-doubt, and even the temptation to quit, you too will encounter obstacles and challenges along the way. The key is to persevere, to stay focused, and to remind yourself of the reasons why you started this journey in the first place.

Just like the players in the Squid Game who had to master a variety of skills to survive – from childhood games like Red Light, Green Light, to intricate tasks like carving a shape out of a honeycomb candy – you too need to equip yourself with the skills that will help you navigate the challenges of life.

Think of those players who excelled at the marble game, not just because of their luck, but because of their strategic thinking, their ability to adapt to changing circumstances, and their willingness to collaborate with others.

These are the skills that can make all the difference in the real world too, yaar. Whether it's negotiating a better salary, managing your finances, or simply communicating effectively with your loved ones, the ability to strategize, adapt, and collaborate can help you overcome any obstacle and achieve your goals.

And just like those players who mastered the art of teamwork during the Tug-of-War game, you too need to build a strong support system, a network of people who will lift you up, challenge you, and help you reach your full potential.

Remember, yaar, life is not a solo game. It's a team effort, a collaborative endeavor where we all need each other's support and encouragement to succeed. So, find your tribe, your mentors, your cheerleaders, and let them be your source of strength and inspiration as you navigate the challenges of life.

But hey, leveling up isn't just about acquiring new skills or building a strong support system. It's also about cultivating the right mindset, the mental fortitude that will help you stay focused, motivated, and resilient in the face of adversity.

Think of those players in the Squid Game who, despite facing unimaginable horrors and life-threatening situations, managed to maintain their hope, their dignity, and their will to survive. They reminded us that even in the darkest of times, the human spirit has an incredible capacity for resilience and perseverance.

Similarly, in the game of life, we too will face setbacks, disappointments, and moments of despair. But it's our ability to bounce back, to learn from our mistakes, and to keep moving forward that will ultimately determine our success.

So, what's the takeaway, yaar? It's simple: Just like in the Squid Game, life throws us challenges that test our resilience, our courage, and our ability to adapt. But unlike the game, we have the power to choose our own ending.

Remember, leveling up isn't about shortcuts or magic tricks. It's about investing in yourself, developing your skills, and cultivating a growth mindset. It's about finding your own unique "cheat codes" to navigate the complexities of life, whether it's mastering a new language, learning a valuable trade, or simply honing your problem-solving skills.

Think of it like that time you were trying to assemble a piece of IKEA furniture, the instructions seemingly written in an alien language. You could have given up in frustration, but instead, you persevered, using your ingenuity and a little bit of "jugaad" to finally put the darn thing together. That sense of accomplishment, that feeling of empowerment, that's what leveling up is all about.

So, yaar, don't be afraid to step out of your comfort zone, to challenge yourself, to learn new things. Embrace the journey of self-improvement, and remember that every skill you acquire, every lesson you learn, is a step closer to achieving your Dalgona dreams.

And just like those players in the Squid Game who formed alliances and helped each other out, remember that you don't have to go it alone. Surround yourself with a supportive tribe, people who believe in you, who encourage you, and who challenge you to be your best.

Whether it's a mentor who guides you, a friend who lends a listening ear, or a family member who offers unconditional love, these connections can be your lifeline, your source of strength and inspiration.

Remember, yaar, we're all in this together. We all have our own unique challenges, our own fears and insecurities. But by supporting each other, by sharing our knowledge and experiences, and by celebrating each other's successes, we can create a community of growth, empowerment, and mutual respect.

So, reach out to your tribe, yaar. Connect with those who inspire you, who motivate you, and who make you believe in yourself. Share your dreams, your goals, and your struggles. And don't be afraid to ask for help when you need it.

Because just like those players in the Squid Game who found strength in numbers, you too can achieve greatness when you have a supportive community by your side.

Remember, leveling up isn't just about individual achievement, it's about collective growth. It's about lifting each other up, inspiring each other, and creating a world where everyone has the opportunity to shine.

And just like those iconic video game characters who level up and unlock new abilities as they progress through the levels, you too have the power to level up your life by pursuing your side quests with dedication, creativity, and a whole lot of "jugaad."

Think of it like Mario collecting those power-up mushrooms, transforming from a humble plumber to a fire-breathing, invincible hero. Or like Link in The Legend of Zelda, acquiring new weapons and skills as he navigates through treacherous dungeons and battles fierce monsters.

Your side quests can be your own personal power-ups, unlocking hidden talents, boosting your confidence, and equipping you with the tools you need to conquer the challenges of life. They can be your secret weapon, your ace in the hole, your path to becoming the best version of yourself.

So, embrace those side quests, yaar. Nurture them with the same dedication and enthusiasm that you bring to your main job or your primary responsibilities. Treat them as opportunities for growth, for learning, for self-discovery.

And most importantly, have fun with them! Let them be a source of joy, excitement, and fulfillment in your life.

Because in the grand adventure of life, it's not just about reaching the final destination, it's about enjoying the journey, discovering hidden treasures along the way, and creating a story that's uniquely yours.

So, go on, my friend. Level up your life, embrace your side quests, and let the world witness your extraordinary journey.

Remember, just as the Squid Game offered unexpected twists and turns, life too is full of surprises. You might stumble upon a hidden passion, discover a talent you never knew you had, or meet someone who inspires you to reach new heights. So, keep your eyes open, your heart open, and your mind open to the endless possibilities that life has to offer.

And just like those players who formed unlikely alliances and friendships in the game, remember the importance of community and connection. Surround yourself with people who lift you up, who believe in you, and who encourage you to pursue your dreams. Because just as iron sharpens iron, so too can the right company help you become the best version of yourself.

So, yaar, whether it's mastering a new skill, pursuing a passion, or simply embracing a growth mindset, remember that leveling up is a continuous process. It's about constantly challenging yourself, learning from your experiences, and striving to become the hero of your own story.

And just like those iconic video game characters who leave a lasting impression on our hearts and minds, let your journey of self-improvement be one that inspires others, that leaves a legacy of growth, resilience, and unwavering determination.

Because in the end, yaar, it's not about the level you reach, it's about the impact you make. It's about living a life that's full of purpose, passion, and a whole lot of "jugaad." So, go out there and level up your life, my friend. The world is waiting for your unique brand of brilliance to shine.

CHAPTER THIRTEEN

BOSS BATTLES: HANDLING DIFFICULT PEOPLE

Picture this, yaar: You're walking down a dark alley, the streetlights flickering ominously, the shadows stretching long and menacing. Suddenly, a figure emerges from the darkness, their eyes glinting with malice, their voice booming with a chilling threat: *"Kitne aadmi the?"* (How many men were there?)

It's Gabbar Singh, the iconic villain from "Sholay," and he's not in a good mood. He's demanding answers, he's flexing his power, and he's making it clear that you're in his territory now.

But fear not, my friend. This isn't a scene from a Bollywood movie, it's a metaphor for the boss battles we all face in life. Those difficult people, the Gabbar Singhs and Mogambos who seem to delight in making our lives miserable, testing our patience, and pushing us to our limits.

Whether it's a tyrannical boss, a manipulative colleague, a nosy neighbor, or even a toxic family member, we all encounter individuals who seem to thrive on conflict, drama, and negativity. They are the thorns in our side, the speed bumps on our road to success, the villains in our own personal Bollywood dramas.

But hey, don't worry, yaar. We're not going to let these Gabbar Singhs and Mogambos of life get the better of us. We're going to channel our inner heroes, our inner Vijay Dinanath Chauhans, and face these boss battles with courage, resilience, and a whole lot of jugaad.

Just like how Seong Gi-hun, our lovable yet flawed protagonist, navigated the treacherous games with a mix of street smarts, compassion, and sheer dumb luck, we too can learn to tackle the "boss battles" of life with our own unique blend of skills and strategies.

Remember that tense moment in the marble game when Gi-hun faced off against the elderly Il-nam? He could have easily taken advantage of the old man's failing memory, but instead, he chose to play fair, to connect with him on a human level, and to ultimately learn a valuable lesson about life and loss.

Similarly, dealing with difficult people doesn't always mean resorting to confrontation or aggression. Sometimes, it's about finding common ground, building bridges of understanding, and appealing to their better nature. Just like Gi-hun, who saw the humanity even in his opponents, we too can try to understand the motivations and insecurities that drive difficult people's behavior.

But hey, let's be real, yaar. Not every Gabbar Singh or Mogambo is going to respond to kindness and understanding. Some people are just plain toxic, manipulative, and downright nasty. And in those cases, it's important to set boundaries, protect yourself, and not let their negativity drag you down.

Remember that scene in the Squid Game where the players had to form teams for the tug-of-war challenge? They had to carefully choose their allies, ensuring a balance of strength, strategy, and trust. Similarly, in the game of life, it's crucial to surround yourself with people who uplift you, support you, and bring out the best in you.

Avoid those energy vampires who drain your enthusiasm, those naysayers who constantly criticize your dreams, and those toxic individuals who thrive on drama and conflict. Just like a weak link in the tug-of-war rope can lead to the entire team's downfall, negative people can drag you down and hinder your progress.

Let's take a trip down memory lane, back to our college days, shall we? Remember our friend, the one and only "Chatterbox" Chhavi? This girl could talk for hours on end, about anything and everything under the sun. She had an opinion on every topic, from the latest Bollywood gossip to the intricacies of quantum physics. And let's not forget her legendary ability to turn any conversation into a full-blown debate, complete with hand gestures, dramatic pauses, and the occasional raised eyebrow.

One day, during a group project, we were brainstorming ideas for a presentation. Chhavi, as usual, was in full flow, passionately advocating for her idea, while the rest of us struggled to get a word in edgewise. Suddenly, in the midst of her monologue, she paused, a look of confusion crossing her face. "Wait a minute," she said, "what were we talking about again?"

We all burst out laughing, the tension in the room instantly dissipating. Chhavi's forgetfulness, her ability to get so caught up in her own thoughts that she lost track of the conversation, was both endearing and hilarious. It was a reminder that even the most eloquent and opinionated among us can have their moments of absent-mindedness.

But more importantly, it taught us a valuable lesson about the importance of listening, of truly hearing what others have to say, even if their opinions differ from our own. It's about respecting different perspectives, being open to new ideas, and recognizing that we don't always have to be the loudest voice in the room.

So, the next time you find yourself in a conversation with a "Chatterbox" Chhavi, don't just tune them out or try to out-talk them. Instead, listen actively, engage with their ideas, and try to see things from their point of view. You might just learn something new, gain a fresh perspective, or even discover a hidden gem of wisdom amidst the chatter.

And remember, yaar, even the most talkative among us have moments of vulnerability, moments when they need a listening ear and a supportive friend. So, be there for your Chhavis, your chatterboxes, your friends who might be struggling with their own inner demons. Offer them your understanding, your empathy, and your unwavering support.

Just like those unsung heroes who work tirelessly behind the scenes of a Bollywood movie, contributing their talents to create a masterpiece, your side quests can be a way to express your creativity, explore your passions, and make a meaningful contribution to the world.

Whether it's volunteering at a local community center, mentoring a young student, or simply lending a helping hand to a neighbor in need, these acts of service can bring a sense of purpose and fulfillment that transcends the daily grind.

Remember, yaar, life is not just about what you achieve for yourself, but also about the impact you make on the lives of others. It's about spreading kindness, sharing your talents, and contributing to the greater good.

Just like those heartwarming Bollywood scenes where the hero selflessly helps others, your side quests can be a way to showcase your own humanity, compassion, and generosity. They can be a reminder that even the smallest acts of kindness can have a ripple effect, creating a positive impact that extends far beyond your own immediate circle.

So, yaar, don't underestimate the power of your side quests. They might not bring you fame or fortune, but they can bring you something far more valuable - a sense of purpose, a feeling of connection, and the satisfaction of knowing that you're making a difference in the world.

Embrace them, nurture them, and let them be a source of joy, inspiration, and fulfillment in your life. Because just like those hidden gems in the bylanes of your city, your side quests might just be the key to unlocking a whole new world of possibilities, a world where you can truly shine and make your mark.

Just like those seemingly impossible levels in video games where you're faced with a formidable boss, life too throws us curveballs in the form of difficult people. These individuals, with their prickly personalities and knack for pushing our buttons, can be as frustrating as a glitchy controller or a buffering internet connection.

They might be the overbearing boss who breathes down your neck, the gossipmonger colleague who spreads rumors faster than a WhatsApp forward, or the know-it-all relative who always has an unsolicited opinion.

These "boss battles" can leave you feeling drained, demotivated, and questioning your own sanity. It's like being stuck in a never-ending game of whack-a-mole, where just when you think you've dealt with one problem, another one pops up.

But fear not, my friend. Just like those seasoned gamers who develop strategies and techniques to defeat even the most challenging bosses, you too can learn to navigate these tricky encounters and emerge victorious.

It's about recognizing their patterns, understanding their motivations, and developing a game plan that allows you to maintain your composure, protect your energy, and ultimately, achieve your goals.

Remember, every boss battle is an opportunity to level up your emotional intelligence, your communication skills, and your overall resilience. So, gear up, my friend, and let's conquer these challenges together, one difficult person at a time.

Take our good ol' friend, Ramesh. Remember how he used to get flustered whenever our professor, Dr. Sharma, fired those rapid-fire questions at him during class? Ramesh, bless his soul, was a brilliant student, but Dr. Sharma's interrogation style would turn him into a stuttering, blushing mess. It was like watching a deer caught in the headlights of a speeding truck - painful, yet strangely hilarious.

One day, tired of being Dr. Sharma's favorite target, Ramesh decided to take matters into his own hands. He spent hours practicing his responses, researching the topics, and even role-playing with his friends. He was determined to face this "boss battle" head-on and emerge victorious.

The next time Dr. Sharma called on him, Ramesh took a deep breath, channeled his inner Shah Rukh Khan, and delivered a flawless answer, complete with witty remarks and insightful observations. Dr. Sharma was visibly impressed, and the rest of the class erupted in applause. Ramesh had not only conquered his fear but also earned the respect of his professor and peers.

Ramesh's story is a reminder that even the most daunting boss battles can be won with the right preparation, mindset, and a dash of humor. It's about recognizing your strengths, addressing your weaknesses, and finding the courage to stand up for yourself.

Similarly, when faced with difficult people in your own life, don't let their negativity or intimidation tactics get the better of you. Take a page from Ramesh's book and arm yourself with knowledge, confidence, and a healthy dose of wit.

Remember, yaar, you don't have to be a victim in these boss battles. You have the power to set boundaries, to assert yourself, and to protect your own well-being. Just like those Bollywood heroes who always find a way to outsmart the villain, you too can find your own "jugaad" to navigate these tricky encounters and emerge victorious. But let's face it, yaar, not every difficult person in our lives is a comical figure like Chatterbox Chhavi or a misguided soul like Dr. Sharma. Some individuals are genuinely toxic, their negativity spreading like wildfire, their words cutting deeper than a Samurai sword.

Think of that colleague who constantly undermines your efforts, that relative who never misses an opportunity to criticize your choices, or that "friend" who always seems to bring you down with their negativity. These individuals can be like the menacing guards in the Squid Game, their presence looming over you, their words and actions threatening to extinguish your spark.

Dealing with such toxic individuals can be emotionally draining and mentally exhausting. It's like walking on eggshells, constantly trying to avoid triggering their wrath or becoming a target of their negativity. It can make you question your own worth, your own sanity, and your own ability to navigate the complexities of human relationships.

But just like those brave players in the Squid Game who found ways to resist the guards' brutality, to protect their allies, and to maintain their dignity amidst the chaos, you too have the power to stand up to toxic individuals and protect your own well-being.

It's not about fighting fire with fire, yaar. It's about setting boundaries, asserting yourself, and refusing to let their negativity dictate your emotions or your actions.

It's about recognizing that you have the right to be treated with respect, to feel safe and valued in your relationships, and to protect your own mental and emotional health.

Let's rewind to our college days. Picture our math professor, the legendary "Calculus King, Dr Verma" who could make even the most complex equations sound like a lullaby. But one day, during a particularly grueling lecture on differential equations, the unexpected happened.

Our friend, the ever-jovial Vikas, decided to break the monotony with a well-timed joke. "Sir," he piped up, "if I differentiate my love for mathematics, will it increase or decrease?"

The entire class erupted in laughter, the tension in the room instantly dissolving. Even the Calculus King couldn't help but crack a smile. It was a reminder that even in the most serious of situations, a touch of humor can go a long way in diffusing tension and building connections.

Similarly, when dealing with difficult people, a bit of lightheartedness can sometimes work wonders. A well-timed joke, a playful remark, or even a self-deprecating comment can disarm even the most hardened cynic and create an opportunity for genuine connection.

Of course, humor isn't always the answer, and it's important to read the room and gauge the situation before cracking a joke. But when used appropriately, it can be a powerful tool for building rapport, diffusing conflict, and navigating those tricky boss battles with a smile on your face.

So, the next time you find yourself facing a difficult person, remember Vikas and his witty remark in math class. Remember that a little bit of humor can go a long way in building bridges, breaking down barriers, and even turning a potential enemy into a friend.

And just like Vikas, who used his humor to connect with his classmates and even win over the Calculus King, you too can use your own unique brand of wit and charm to navigate the challenges of life and emerge victorious.

It's about understanding that while we can't control the actions of others, we can control our own responses. We can choose to rise above the negativity, to maintain our composure, and to focus on the things that truly matter.

Just like those players in the Squid Game who learned to adapt and strategize in the face of danger, we too can develop coping mechanisms to deal with difficult people. It might be setting boundaries, practicing assertive communication, or simply learning to walk away from toxic situations.

Remember, yaar, you don't have to engage in every battle. Sometimes, the wisest move is to simply disengage, to protect your energy, and to focus on your own well-being. Just like a skilled chess player who knows when to sacrifice a pawn to protect their queen, you too need to prioritize your own mental and emotional health.

And just like those underdog heroes in Bollywood movies who always find a way to outsmart the villain, you too can find creative solutions to deal with difficult people. It might be using humor to diffuse a tense situation, finding common ground to build a bridge of understanding, or simply setting clear boundaries to protect your own space.

But most importantly, yaar, remember that you're not alone in this. We all have our own Gabbar Singhs and Mogambos to deal with, our own boss battles to fight. But with the right mindset, the right strategies, and a supportive tribe by your side, you can navigate these challenges with grace, resilience, and a whole lot of jugaad.

So, the next time you encounter a difficult person, take a deep breath, channel your inner hero, and remember that you have the power to choose your own response. You can either let their negativity consume you, or you can rise above it, maintain your composure, and continue on your path towards your Dalgona dreams.

Because in the end, yaar, it's not about winning every battle, it's about winning the war. And the war, my friend, is against negativity, self-doubt, and those who try to dim your light. So, go out there and shine brightly, yaar. The world is waiting for your unique brand of brilliance.

And just as every superhero needs a trusty sidekick, every hero in the real-life battlefield of difficult people needs a support system. These are the people who understand your struggles, offer a listening ear, and remind you of your worth when you're feeling down. They're the ones who make you laugh, lift your spirits, and remind you that you're not alone in this fight.

Just like the heartwarming camaraderie among the players in the Squid Game, despite the cutthroat competition, your tribe can be a source of strength and solace in the face of difficult people. They can offer a fresh perspective, help you strategize, and remind you that you're not defined by the negativity of others.

So, reach out to your friends, your family, your mentors, or even a therapist if you need to. Share your experiences, vent your frustrations, and seek their guidance and support. Remember, yaar, it takes a village to raise a child, and it takes a tribe to conquer a boss battle.

But ultimately, yaar, the most powerful weapon in your arsenal against difficult people is your own self-belief. It's that inner voice that tells you, "I am worthy of respect. I deserve to be treated with kindness. I will not let anyone dim my light."

It's about recognizing your own value, setting healthy boundaries, and refusing to be a victim of someone else's negativity. It's about standing tall, speaking your truth, and walking away from situations that compromise your well-being.

Remember, you are the hero of your own story, the master of your own destiny. You have the power to choose your battles, to protect your energy, and to create a life that's filled with positivity, joy, and meaningful connections.

So, the next time you encounter a difficult person, remember the lessons you've learned, the strategies you've developed, and the strength you've cultivated. Face that boss battle with confidence, resilience, and a whole lot of jugaad. And just like those Bollywood heroes who always emerge victorious, you too can conquer any challenge and continue on your path towards your Dalgona dreams.

Think about that one relative, the one who always seems to have a comment about your life choices, your career, your weight, even your choice of haircut. They might mean well, but their constant nitpicking and unsolicited advice can be as irritating as a mosquito buzzing around your ear on a hot summer night.

It's like that uncle at every family gathering who corners you and starts grilling you about your love life, your salary, and your plans for the future, all while you're trying to enjoy a plate of biryani and avoid eye contact with your crush. Or that aunt who insists on feeding you laddoos even though you're trying to watch your waistline.

Dealing with these "well-meaning" but ultimately annoying relatives can be a challenge, especially when you're trying to maintain your composure and avoid a family feud that could rival the Mahabharata. But just like those Bollywood heroes who always manage to charm their way out of tricky situations with a witty remark or a disarming smile, you too can learn to navigate these encounters with grace and humor.

It'might be a playful retort, a gentle deflection, or simply a change of subject. The key is to not take their comments personally, to recognize that their behavior often stems from their own insecurities or anxieties, and to respond with kindness and understanding, even if it's through gritted teeth.

Remember, yaar, you don't have to let their negativity dampen your spirits or derail your dreams. Just like those Bollywood heroines who always manage to win over their disapproving in-laws with their wit and charm, you too can navigate these tricky family dynamics with a smile on your face and a twinkle in your eye.

Or that time when our hostel warden, the infamous "Hitler Uncle," caught us red-handed sneaking in a late-night pizza party. We were trembling in our pajamas, expecting the worst. But instead of unleashing his wrath, Hitler Uncle surprised us all. He calmly walked into the room, sniffed the air, and said, "Smells like a party! Mind if I join?"

We were stunned, but also relieved. And guess what? That night turned into an epic pizza-fueled bonding session, where we shared stories, laughter, and even a few dance moves with the warden we had feared for so long.

It was a reminder that sometimes, the most difficult people can surprise us with their humanity, their sense of humor, and their willingness to connect on a deeper level. It's about finding those moments of unexpected connection, those shared experiences that can bridge the gap between us and even transform a potential boss battle into a heartwarming memory.

So, the next time you find yourself facing a difficult person, don't give up on them too quickly. Give them a chance, try to see things from their perspective, and look for opportunities to connect on a human level.

You might just discover a hidden side to them, a softer, kinder, more relatable side that you never knew existed. And who knows, you might even end up sharing a pizza and a few laughs with your own "Hitler Uncle."

But here's the thing, yaar. It's not just about dealing with difficult people, it's also about understanding them, and sometimes, even empathizing with them. Remember Gabbar Singh's backstory in "Sholay"? It revealed a troubled past, a childhood filled with hardship and injustice, that shaped his hardened personality and fueled his thirst for revenge.

Similarly, those difficult people we encounter in our lives might be battling their own inner demons, carrying burdens that we can't even fathom. It's easy to label them as "toxic" or "difficult," but perhaps they're simply reacting to their own pain, their own insecurities, or their own unresolved traumas.

This doesn't mean you should excuse their behavior or become a doormat for their negativity. But it does mean that you can approach these "boss battles" with a bit more compassion and understanding.

Just like those Bollywood movies that often show the villain's backstory, revealing their motivations and vulnerabilities, try to see the human being behind the difficult behavior. It might not excuse their actions, but it can help you navigate the situation with more empathy and less frustration.

Maybe that colleague who constantly undermines you is struggling with their own insecurities and feels threatened by your success. Perhaps that relative who criticizes your choices is simply projecting their own unfulfilled dreams onto you. And that "friend" who always seems to bring you down might be grappling with their own demons, using negativity as a coping mechanism.

By understanding their underlying motivations, you can approach these encounters with a more compassionate lens. You can set boundaries without being confrontational, offer support without enabling their behavior, and ultimately, find a way to co-exist peacefully, even if it means maintaining a healthy distance.

Because in the grand tapestry of life, it's not just about the battles we fight or the obstacles we overcome. It's also about the connections we forge, the friendships we nurture, and the love we share. Just like those heartwarming scenes in "Kabhi Khushi Kabhie Gham" where the Raichand family finally reunites after years of separation, or the unbreakable bond between the three friends in "Dil Chahta Hai," our relationships can be a source of immense joy, support, and unconditional love.

So, cherish those bonds, yaar. Invest in your friendships, nurture your family ties, and surround yourself with people who uplift you, inspire you, and make you feel like you belong. Because in the end, it's the love and connection we share with others that truly makes life worth living.

And as you journey through life's ups and downs, remember that you're not alone. Just like those brave players in the Squid Game who formed alliances and helped each other survive, you too have a tribe, a community, a network of people who are rooting for you.

Reach out to them, lean on them, and let them be your source of strength and encouragement. Because just like a strong foundation supports a towering building, a strong support system can help you weather any storm and achieve your dreams.

So, yaar, as you continue to navigate the boss battles of life, remember that you're not just fighting for yourself. You're fighting for your loved ones, for your dreams, and for the kind of world you want to create.

And just like those iconic Bollywood dialogues that leave a lasting impression, let this be your battle cry: "Haar ke jeetne wale ko baazigar kehte hain!" (The one who wins after losing is called a true champion).

Because in the end, yaar, it's not about avoiding the challenges or escaping the difficult people. It's about facing them head-on, with courage, resilience, and a whole lot of jugaad. It's about turning those boss battles into opportunities for growth, for self-discovery, and for creating a life that's truly yours.

We all carry our own burdens, our own past traumas, and our own insecurities. Sometimes, those difficult people we encounter might be reacting to their own pain, their own struggles, or their own unresolved issues.

This doesn't mean you should excuse their behavior or become a doormat for their negativity. But it does mean that you can approach these "boss battles" with a bit more compassion and understanding.

Try to see the human being behind the difficult behavior. It might not excuse their actions, but it can help you navigate the situation with more empathy and less frustration.

By understanding their underlying motivations, you can approach these encounters with a more compassionate lens. You can set boundaries without being confrontational, offer support without enabling their behavior, and ultimately, find a way to co-exist peacefully, even if it means maintaining a healthy distance.

CHAPTER FOURTEEN

THE FINAL ROUND: LIVING A LIFE YOU'RE PROUD OF

Standing at the finish line, the cheers of the crowd echoing in your ears, the medals glistening in the sunlight. You've overcome countless obstacles, faced fierce competitors, and pushed yourself to the very limits. But this isn't just any race, this is the marathon of life, and you've finally reached the final round.

But hold on, my friend, before you start popping the champagne and basking in the glory, let me ask you this: Are you truly proud of the race you ran? Did you stay true to your values, your passions, and your dreams? Or did you compromise along the way, sacrificing your happiness for the sake of external validation or societal expectations?

Because, yaar, the final round of life isn't just about crossing the finish line. It's about the journey you took to get there, the choices you made, the impact you had on the world, and the person you became along the way.

Think of it like that final scene in a classic sports movie, where the underdog athlete, battered and bruised, crosses the finish line not just to win the race, but to prove something to themselves, to the world, and to the naysayers who doubted them.

It's not just about the trophy, the medal, or the accolades. It's about the grit, the determination, the unwavering spirit that carried them through the toughest of times. It's about the lessons they learned, the friendships they forged, and the personal growth they experienced along the way.

Similarly, the final round of your life isn't just about achieving your goals or fulfilling your dreams. It's about living a life that's authentically yours, a life that reflects your values, your passions, and your unique contribution to the world.

It's about looking back on your journey with a sense of pride, knowing that you stayed true to yourself, that you made a difference, and that you left the world a little bit better than you found it.

Just like Player 067, Kang Sae-byeok, the North Korean defector who entered the Squid Game with the sole purpose of winning enough money to reunite her family, we too can be driven by a powerful purpose that fuels our journey. Despite the grim reality of the game, Sae-byeok never lost sight of her goal, her determination unwavering even in the face of unimaginable danger.

Her story reminds us that having a clear purpose, a driving force that motivates us to overcome challenges, can be a powerful tool in creating a fulfilling life. Whether it's reuniting with loved ones, making a difference in the world, or simply living a life of passion and purpose, having a clear "why" can help us navigate the inevitable obstacles and stay focused on our ultimate goals.

So, as you contemplate your own ending, ask yourself, "What is my 'why'? What is that burning desire within me that fuels my dreams and aspirations?" It could be a personal goal, a social cause, or simply a deep-seated longing for a life that's meaningful and fulfilling.

Once you identify your "why," let it be your guiding light, your North Star, as you navigate the challenges and uncertainties of life. Let it be the fire that fuels your passion, the compass that points you in the right direction, and the anchor that keeps you grounded when the storms of life threaten to derail you.

Chapter 15: The Final Round: Living a Life You're Proud Of - Picture Abhi Baaki Hai, Mere Dost (The picture is not over yet, my friend!)

Remember those final exams in college, yaar? The sleepless nights, the endless cups of chai, the frantic cramming sessions that left your brain feeling like a pressure cooker about to explode. It was like being in the final round of the Squid Game, where one wrong move could mean the difference between success and failure, between a bright future and a life of regret.

But amidst all the stress and anxiety, there were also moments of camaraderie, laughter, and shared struggle. Like that time our entire hostel floor gathered in the common room for a marathon study session, fueled by Maggi noodles and endless cups of coffee. We quizzed each other, shared notes, and even cracked a few jokes to ease the tension.

Or that time our friend, the perpetually optimistic Priya, organized a group meditation session to help us calm our nerves before the big day. We sat cross-legged on the floor, chanting Mantras and trying our best to silence the mental chatter. It might not have turned us into Zen masters, but it definitely helped us find a moment of peace amidst the chaos.

These memories, yaar, are a reminder that even in the most challenging of times, there's always room for connection, for laughter, and for shared experiences. It's about finding those moments of joy, those pockets of light that remind us that life is not just about the destination, it's about the journey.

And just like those final exams that tested our knowledge, skills, and resilience, the final round of life is also a test, a culmination of all the lessons we've learned, the experiences we've had, and the choices we've made along the way.

It's a moment of reckoning, a time to reflect on your choices, your achievements, and the legacy you want to leave behind. It's a time to ask yourself, "Have I lived a life that I'm proud of? Have I made a positive impact on the world? Have I fulfilled my potential and chased my dreams?"

Just like those players in the Squid Game who faced their final moments with a mix of regret, acceptance, and hope, we too must confront our own mortality and the finite nature of our time on this planet.

It's a humbling realization, a reminder that life is precious, that time is fleeting, and that we should make the most of every moment.

But instead of succumbing to fear or despair, let this realization be a catalyst for action, a motivation to live a life that's meaningful and purposeful. Let it be a reminder to cherish every moment, to express your love and gratitude to those you care about, and to make a positive impact on the world, no matter how small.

Because in the end, yaar, it's not about the number of years you live, but the quality of life you lead. It's about the memories you create, the connections you forge, and the legacy you leave behind.

So, as you approach the final round of your life's game, remember that you have the power to write your own ending. You can choose to live a life of regret, dwelling on missed opportunities and unfulfilled dreams. Or you can choose to embrace the present moment, to seize every opportunity, and to create a life that's filled with joy, purpose, and a whole lot of "jugaad."

Picture this, yaar: It's the night before our final exams, and the hostel is buzzing with a nervous energy. Students are huddled in groups, cramming last-minute notes, fueled by caffeine and the fear of impending doom. Amidst the chaos, our friend Rahul, the eternal optimist, decides to lighten the mood. He bursts into the common room, wearing a superhero cape and a pair of mismatched socks, declaring himself the "Exam Buster."

"Fear not, my fellow scholars!" he proclaims, striking a dramatic pose. "For I, Rahul the Magnificent, have the ultimate cheat code to ace these exams!"

We all roll our eyes, but can't help but grin at his antics.

"Behold!" he continues, pulling out a dog-eared copy of "The Alchemist" by Paulo Coelho. "This, my friends, is the key to our success. It's a tale of following your dreams, a testament to the power of perseverance, and a reminder that even the most challenging of exams can be conquered with a little bit of magic and a whole lot of heart."

We burst into laughter, the tension in the room melting away. Rahul's infectious enthusiasm and unwavering optimism were a breath of fresh air amidst the exam-induced stress.

Remember that time during our college days, when our friend, the ever-studious and perpetually anxious Rajeev, decided to overcome his fear of public speaking by joining the debate club? We all thought he was crazy. Rajeev, who could barely string a sentence together without blushing, was going to face a room full of strangers and argue his point?

The first few debates were rough, to say the least. Rajeev would stumble over his words, his voice would crack, and he'd often forget his arguments mid-sentence. But instead of giving up, he kept practicing, kept pushing himself, and slowly but surely, his confidence grew.

One day, during a particularly heated debate on the merits of arranged marriages versus love marriages, Rajeev surprised us all. He stood tall, his voice booming with conviction, and delivered a passionate argument that left the audience spellbound. He even managed to crack a few jokes, drawing laughter and applause from the crowd.

We were all amazed, even the usually stoic debate club president couldn't help but grin. Rajeev had not only conquered his fear of public speaking, but he had also discovered a hidden talent for oratory and persuasion.

His story is a reminder that sometimes, the greatest challenges can lead to the most unexpected breakthroughs. It's about pushing your limits, stepping out of your comfort zone, and discovering hidden strengths and talents that you never knew you possessed.

So, the next time you feel like you're stuck in a rut, or that you're not good enough, remember Rajeev and his triumphant debate performance. Remember that you too have the power to overcome your fears, to unleash your hidden potential, and to level up your life in ways you never imagined possible.

But even in the realm of self-improvement, there's always room for a good laugh, yaar. Just think back to that time when our friend, the fitness enthusiast Vikram, decided to try his hand at yoga. Picture him, all decked out in his brand-new yoga pants and a matching headband, attempting a downward dog pose.

Let's just say, it wasn't exactly a picture of grace and flexibility. More like a clumsy puppy trying to scratch its back on a carpet. We couldn't help but burst into laughter as Vikram struggled to maintain his balance, his limbs contorted in ways that defied all laws of human anatomy.

But you know what? Vikram didn't give up. He laughed along with us, dusted himself off, and tried again. And again. And again. And eventually, with practice and perseverance, he mastered that downward dog, along with a few other impressive asanas.

Vikram's story is a lighthearted reminder that the journey of self-improvement is not always a smooth one. There will be stumbles, fumbles, and moments of utter hilarity. But as long as you approach it with a sense of humor, a willingness to laugh at yourself, and an unwavering determination to succeed, you'll eventually reach your goals.

So, yaar, don't take yourself too seriously. Embrace the awkwardness, the missteps, and the occasional face-plants along the way. Remember, even the most successful people have had their share of embarrassing moments. It's what makes us human, it's what makes life interesting, and it's what adds a touch of spice to our personal growth journeys.

So, what's the takeaway, yaar? It's simple: Just like in the Squid Game, life throws us challenges that test our resilience, our courage, and our ability to adapt. But unlike the game, we have the power to choose our own ending.

Remember, leveling up isn't about shortcuts or magic tricks. It's about investing in yourself, developing your skills, and cultivating a growth mindset. It's about finding your own unique "cheat codes" to navigate the complexities of life, whether it's mastering a new language, learning a valuable trade, or simply honing your problem-solving skills.

Think of it like that time you were trying to assemble a piece of furniture, the instructions seemingly written in an alien language. You could have given up in frustration, but instead, you persevered, using your ingenuity and a little bit of "jugaad" to finally put the darn thing together. That sense of accomplishment, that feeling of empowerment, that's what leveling up is all about.

So, yaar, don't be afraid to step out of your comfort zone, to challenge yourself, to learn new things. Embrace the journey of self-improvement, and remember that every skill you acquire, every lesson you learn, is a step closer to achieving your Dalgona dreams.

So, yaar, let's make a pact. Let's promise to be kind to ourselves, to forgive our mistakes, to celebrate our victories, no matter how small. Let's silence that inner critic and embrace our inner strengths.

Remember, the game of marbles of self-love is not about winning or losing. It's about playing with an open heart, embracing the ups and downs, and learning to love yourself unconditionally. Because when you truly love yourself, you'll find that you have the power to achieve anything you set your mind to.

So, go on, yaar. Take that leap of faith, chase those dreams, and live a life that's authentically yours. And remember, just as the most inspiring stories leave us with a message of hope and strength, let the story of your life be a masterpiece filled with love, laughter, and unapologetic self-expression.

Because at the end of the day, my friend, you are not just a player in this game of life. You are the hero, the champion, the one who gets to write their own ending.

Aur haan, ek aur baat (And yes, one more thing): Don't forget to share your story with the world. Your journey of self-love might just be the inspiration someone else needs to start their own. So, go on, spread the love, and let's create a world where everyone feels like apni favourite.

So, what's the takeaway, yaar? It's simple: Just like in the Squid Game, life throws us challenges that test our resilience, our courage, and our ability to adapt. But unlike the game, we have the power to choose our own ending.

Remember, leveling up isn't about shortcuts or magic tricks. It's about investing in yourself, developing your skills, and cultivating a growth mindset. It's about finding your own unique "cheat codes" to navigate the complexities of life, whether it's mastering a new language, learning a valuable trade, or simply honing your problem-solving skills.

Think of it like that time you were trying to assemble a piece of furniture, the instructions seemingly written in an alien language. You could have given up in frustration, but instead, you persevered, using your ingenuity and a little bit of "jugaad" to finally put the darn thing together. That sense of accomplishment, that feeling of empowerment, that's what leveling up is all about.

Just like every great story, your life too deserves a fitting climax, an ending that leaves a lasting impression. It's the final chapter, the grand finale, the moment where you look back on your journey and say, "Picture abhi baaki hai, mere dost!" (The picture is not over yet, my friend!)

But what does that mean, yaar? What does a fulfilling ending look like in the grand tapestry of life? It's not just about reaching a certain age, accumulating wealth, or achieving external success. It's about something far more profound, something that resonates with your soul and leaves a legacy that transcends time.

Imagine yourself in your twilight years, sitting on a porch swing, sipping a cup of chai, and reflecting on the life you've lived. What memories bring a smile to your face? What experiences fill your heart with warmth and gratitude? What stories do you want to share with your grandchildren, your legacy to the world?

Perhaps you'll recall that time you took a leap of faith and pursued your passion, despite the naysayers and the doubts. You'll remember the struggles, the setbacks, and the moments of self-doubt, but you'll also remember the thrill of overcoming challenges, the joy of creating something meaningful, and the satisfaction of living a life that's authentically yours.

Or maybe you'll think back to the friendships you've nurtured, the bonds you've forged, and the love you've shared with those closest to your heart. You'll remember the laughter, the tears, the shared experiences that have shaped your life and made it so rich and colorful.

You might also reflect on the impact you've made on the world, the lives you've touched, and the difference you've made, no matter how small. It could be the kindness you showed to a stranger, the support you offered to a friend in need, or the passion you poured into your work.

Whatever your story may be, let it be one that you're proud of, yaar. Let it be a story that inspires others, that uplifts their spirits, and that reminds them of the beauty, resilience, and infinite possibilities of the human spirit.

Because in the end, that's what truly matters. It's not the number of years you live, but the quality of life you lead. It's not about the destination, but the journey. And it's up to you to make it a journey that's worth remembering, a journey that leaves a lasting legacy, a journey that says, "I lived my life to the fullest, I embraced the challenges, I loved with all my heart, and I made a difference in the world."

So, as you approach the final round of your life's game, remember that the picture is not over yet, my friend. There's still time to create new memories, to forge new connections, and to leave your mark on the world.

To *Mom*,
For always believing in me, even when I didn't believe
in myself.